TREEHOUSES

TREEHOUSES

View From the Top

John Harris

DEDICATION

To Suzanne McGruther. Her dedication in researching this book, dexterity with the written word, and ability to become entwined in the lives of the many treehouse owners featured in this book made it come alive.

Also to The TreeHouse Company team: designers Gordon Brown and Mark Waterfield; Carole Calderwood, and Anne Bryden in accounts, operations, and sales; but mainly to the treehouse builders who make it all happen—Willie McCubbin, Jim Wales, Brian Keown, Stuart Carmichael, Paul Templeman, Peter Beetschen, Derek Ross, Derek Saunderson, Peter Tudhope, Dax Druce, Gerry Sollitt, Henry Durham, George Grossart, and Paul Cran.

To my wife Moira and her endless patience and my two boys on the left who started it all, Ross and Fraser.

With thanks to Sadolin Woodstains—"Trees need bark, wood needs Sadolin"—and to my many clients—now friends—who have inspired me and helped in the development of The TreeHouse Company, in particular Prof. David Norburn, Felix Dennis, Peter Fowler, Iain Sharp, and of course the Price family.

John Harris

www.treehouse-company.com

First Lyons Press Edition 2003

Produced by PRC Publishing Limited,
The Chrysalis Building
Bramley Road, London W10 6SP
An imprint of **Chrysalis** Books Group plc

The Lyons Press is an imprint of The Globe Pequot Press

10 9 8 7 6 5 4 3 2 1

ISBN 1-59228-155-9

Library Of Congress Cataloging-in-Publication data is available on file

Printed in Malaysia

CONTENTS

INTRODUCTION

Climbing trees is a childhood tradition. And where there are trees and humans, there have always been treehouses—places to sleep, to eat, to dream, and to play.

Opposite page: High in the treetops of Irian Jaya, in Papua New Guinea, live a tribe of reputed cannibals called the Korowai. Protecting them from other warring tribes, their treehouses are also used as homes.

Above: Treehouses have been most common in the South Pacific such as this observation post in the Malay archipelago.

Our most distant ancestors were tree-dwellers, living in the heights safe from prowling animals and flood-waters. Throughout history there are fascinating worldwide accounts of the building of homes in the tree-tops, and, as you will see in this book treehouses are even more popular than ever today, serving as hotel rooms, secret hideaways, dining rooms, and even a conference center.

It is easy to forget though, that a treehouse is dependent upon its host, the tree. If it weren't for the singing birds, swaying branches, and the shady canopy, a treehouse would be nothing more than another garden shed. Looking back on the history of the world, trees have been worshiped by various religions and exalted for their utility in everyday life. It's hard to imagine our planet without them, and yet in the modern world we take little notice of them. As the Western world has come all too late to realize, we need our precious trees to sustain life on this Earth. Among the many advantages of owning a treehouse—the wonderful view, the peace and serenity, the place for the children to escape to—perhaps the best is that it brings you so close to the living host; its seasons, its smell, and the life in its branches.

In an age when treehouses have become so fashionable to own, their building has to be conducted respectfully with sound environmental principles, using wood from sustainable sources and without damaging trees. Once built, a treehouse will give its owners the opportunity to claim a unique place in their lives. With living wood beneath their feet and their back to a tree trunk, they will discover a sense of peace that is lacking in modern culture—a space to slow down from a busy life and simply breathe and think.

Treehouses are traditionally thought of in the West as being a part of the realm of childhood and when we grow up we are expected to lose this innocent connection with our trees. Parents may spend hours crafting a wooden house in the branches for their little ones, but once finished, the sign on the door will read "Adults No Entry!" It is no

coincidence that treehouses are vacated at the same time as childhood stories of Tarzan, The Swiss Family Robinson, and Winnie-the-Pooh are discarded. Literature re-enforces the idea that treehouses are just for kids. Even Anne of Green Gables, the ultimate literary romantic, eventually grew out of her "Idlewild" treehouse.

Trees are most often seen as magical only in children's stories, where they are inhabited by characters like Robin Hood, who lives in a tree in Sherwood Forest with his merry men, or the eternally young Peter Pan, who decides to live with Tinkerbell among the fairy nests in the treetops of Neverland. Indeed, many fantastical treehouses exist in literature, such as the houses occupied by Winnie-the-Pooh's friends in the Hundred Acre Wood. In J.R.R. Tolkien's *The Lord of the Rings*, the Elven tree-dwellers, the Galadhrim, reach their tree-platforms in the yellow-leaved mallorn-trees by rope-ladders.

"It is told that she had a house built in the branches of a tree that grew near the falls; for that is the custom of the Elves of Lorien, to dwell in the trees, and maybe it is so still—even in these latter days dwelling in the trees might be thought safer than sitting on the ground."

The Lord of the Rings

There is however, at least one encouraging fable written about an adult who spends his whole life in the trees. *The Baron in the Trees*, written by Italo Calvino in the 1950s, portrays a young Italian noble-man called Cosimo, who as an adolescent is dispirited by the prospect of a stifling future of courtly manners in polite society. By deciding to spend his entire life in the treetops of the forests of Ombrosa, the Baron is able to converse with the lowest and greatest of mankind, while always being irrevocably tied to his beloved trees and the crea-tures that dwell with him. While most adults would not want to live

Right: Designed and constructed by The TreeHouse Company, this treehouse hotel suite, looking like a set from *Lord of the Rings* was built in the grounds of Fernie castle in Fife.

Left: The treehouse at Cobham Hall
where Queen Elizabeth I banqueted.

Left: The treehouse at Cobham Hall
where Queen Elizabeth I banqueted.

Right: This Medicean treehouse at
Pratolino, near Florence has jetting
fountains, a spiral stairway, and marble
decorations.

permanently in the trees, the Baron's tale shows a desire for an escape from our manmade world of bricks and mortar that is common for many ordinary grown-up citizens today.

It is usually those adults who have grown up with the literary descriptions of treehouse living who secretly most want to recreate that bygone experience. Where children long to be older and able to do all the things their elders can, adults tend to look back upon their childhood as a special time that is gone and lost forever. It takes an open mind and a bit of courage to try to recapture that sense of childhood freedom. Grown-up treehouse owners are often misperceived as being New Age tree-huggers, and their family and friends are sometimes skeptical about the idea of having a treehouse. Yet like any outdoor building, you make of it what you will. If you have grown out of believing in magic, your treehouse can simply be used a practical extra living space or a hip design feature to add to your home. It can be a home office, an artist's garret, or an artistic statement. It can also be subversive, as in the numerous cases of protesters who have built platforms in endangered woods to try to stop the earthmovers. Yet for those who still have a bit of childhood running in their veins, the idea of swaying gently in a room in the trees is a connection to the sense of wonder that was put aside of many years previously. Many an adult has built a treehouse supposedly for their children or grandchildren, only to enjoy occupying it themselves. Famous adults who have built treehouses include John Lennon, who reputedly had one overlooking the Strawberry Fields Orphanage, and Winston Churchill, who constructed a treehouse twenty feet up in a lime tree at his home in Chartwell, near Westerham, England.

Look further back in time, though, and you will discover just how rich the history of treehouse building has been. Accounts of treetop dwellers stretch far back to the South Sea islands where thatched treehouses were widespread throughout the region. These were secure dwelling homes, with baskets woven from plant fibers used to lower people up and down the tree trunks. Captain Cook recorded meetings in the 1700s with native Tasmanians who were living in the trees. In the East, the Japanese have had a long history of building walkways through the trees to give a bird's eye view of their gardens. And even today there are tribes still in existence who live high in homes in the trees of Irian Jaya, Papua New Guinea.

Treehouses have also been much loved by the rich and powerful of society. In Persia, the nobility would ascend stairways into the trees where they had designed luxurious platforms to shade them under the leafy canopy, decorated with gold and silver, and with cooling water provided by fountains.

Caligula, the notorious Roman emperor, was famous for his eccentric behavior, such as drinking pearls dissolved in vinegar and planning to appoint his horse a priest of the temple. However, he showed a great deal of wisdom in having a treehouse built, which he called his "Eyrie," in a giant plane tree. Here he would bring up to fifteen guests, who could lounge on benches arranged on the shady branches. Servants provided extravagant feasts of ostrich, flamingo, and parrot, which were washed down with silver bowls full of honeyed wine, while dancers, jugglers, and acrobats balanced up the tree, attempting to entertain the party.

Caligula's arboreal retreat was perhaps in inspiration to the opulent Medici dukes who resided in Italy some fifteen centuries later. The Renaissance had brought about a renewed interest in everything Classical, and the treehouse became an essential must-have item in Florentine garden architecture. Cosimo I commissioned the architect Tribolo to build him a treehouse in a huge holm oak in the grounds of his home at Villa Castello. Chronicler Vasari described the treehouse at Villa Castello as being "so thickly covered with ivy that it looked like a thicket." It also boasted an incredible series of pipes and taps that spouted water through the air. Cosimo's son, Francesco, was not to be outdone by his father and commissioned his own treehouse at Villa Pratolino, called "The Fountain of the Oak." It had two massive

spiral staircases reaching to a platform twenty-five feet from the ground, set with a large marble table and, of course, fountains.

Unfortunately these fabulous treehouses are long gone, but one tiny tearoom treehouse remains, held in the branches of an oak at Villa Petraia, near Florence. It is here that King Vittorio Emanuele II used to meet with his mistress.

The British nobility also discovered the pleasures of whiling away the hours under a shady canopy. Britain is the home of one of the oldest treehouses still in existence. Pitchford Hall, situated on private land near Acton Burnell in Shropshire, has a small Grade A historical listed building marked at its location on the British ordnance survey map. "The Tree with a House in it," is a small habitation constructed around 1560 for the Ottley family, who then resided at the hall. Resting in the arms of a 500-year-old lime tree, the Tudor-look

treehouse was built with the same care and to the same quality as a proper house of the time would have been. It has endured remarkably well, having been renovated in the latter part of the eighteenth century. The windows and doors were rebuilt with ogee heading, and the fine Chippendale plasterwork enriched with Rococo-Gothic motifs, including a ceiling rose of a female face. More recently, in the 1970s, the treehouse was propped using stilts to ensure that it would remain safe. The longevity of its presence alone would ensure a historical listing, however, this treehouse is also recorded in the diaries of Queen Victoria, who visited Pitchford Hall as a young Princess. She wrote of her stay on the estate, that after a Sunday morning at church, her party returned to the hall to tour the grounds, where she "went up a staircase to a little house in a tree."

The treehouses being built today are adding to a long history rather than being a radical new invention. You would be forgiven for assuming, however, that actually working in your own treehouse office is a new idea that has much to do with escaping from the modern rat-race. In actual fact, people have been recognizing trees as the perfect host for working life since the Middle Ages, when Franciscan monks would use very basic little tree-rooms as a retreat where they could laboriously copy out their manuscripts and meditate in a peaceful atmosphere. Likewise, Hindu monks would reside in tree hermitages, freed from earthbound considerations. In Britain, in 1785, on Worlington Common, Suffolk, there was a cobbler's shop in a tree. Today, you will find a special treehouse for home-schoolers in North America, a conference treehouse in the north of Scotland, and numerous tree-offices for business people, artists, and crafts-folk throughout the world.

Looking through the examples in this book of treehouses built for dining and entertaining, you might also assume that the idea of eating in the treetops is a new fad. However, there is an immensely rich tradition of treehouse feasting that stretches even further back than Caligula's banquets, to ancient China, where there are records of platforms having been raised up trees and used as dining places. The most famous European example, though, is that of the restaurants dubbed "Les Robinsons," at Plessy Robinson, eight miles west of Paris. From 1848 onward, until they were destroyed last century, this was where chic Parisians spent their Sundays. The brainwave of a publican, Joseph Greusquin, the restaurants were built in

Above: This historic building in Shropshire is Britain's oldest remaining treehouse, resting in a 500-year-old lime tree. It was made famous by Queen Victoria's visit to Pitchford Hall as a young girl. She recorded the event in her personal diary.

Left: A modern day treehouse and deck built in two oak trees next to a pond in Shropshire, England.

L. Baslé phot.-édit., Robinson (Seine)

Above: **From 1848 until the middle of last century, numerous dining-table nests were perched in the trees of Plessy-Robinson, near Paris. Used by chic locals, the eateries were serviced by waiters who would bring food on a tray to the base of the tree trunk, and hoist up the meal by basket pulley.**

Above right: Le Chene Classé. The Monument Oak with the twin chapels at Notre Dame de la Paix at Allouville, Normandy, France.

chestnut trees covered in rambling roses. A popular meal was roast chicken and champagne; each course hoisted up by the guests in a basket pulley. At the height of its popularity, there were 200 tables available, and after eating the Parisians were encouraged to stay and play boules or dance to the music of the accordion player. Plessy Robinson was also a popular venue for hosting family celebrations, in particular weddings.

Recently, the treetop wedding has been rediscovered in North America, where in 1997 Ron and Michelle Culley, residents of New York State, tied the knot. Michelle put on her wedding dress inside the treehouse that she and her husband-to-be had built together, and descended its twenty-two steps to be married in the garden below.

Today, treehouse tourism is splendidly rife, with luxury resorts in Puerto Rico, Hainan Island in China, and Hue Province in Vietnam. You can stay at the "House of the August Moon" in an African tulip tree in Hawaii, with ocean views lit by tiki torches, or spend the night in "The Kingfisher Treehouse" in Green Turtle Bay in the Bahamas, surrounded by azure waters and hibiscus flowers. You can dine in a treehouse balcony with the possums in the hinterland of Queensland's Sunshine Coast, complete with in-house massage and room service. Even Northern Kerala in India offers accommodation ninety feet up in tropical rainforest amid pepper and cardamom plantations, just so long as you can stand the height!

Treehouses can be found in the most unexpected and secret places on Earth. I've been told of a hollowed out tree that was used as a ticket office on Britain's Great Western Railway last century; of a cyber café found two hours from civilization in Southern Turkey, high in the treetops; of an oak tree fused with a church in Normandy called "Le Chene Classé," that has been used as a chapel for over 800 years.

Treehouses are never far away—ask around. There's probably one in your town, hidden above your head amid the leaves.

The TreeHouse Company have been adding to the map of treehouses in Britain and throughout Europe over the last few years. While there have been many amateur treehouses constructed, and some magnificent examples from history of elaborate tree-dwellings, there has certainly not been a professional company devoted solely to treehouse construction until recent times.

Above right: A shaped door between the two main boughs of this majestic beech tree gives a sense of magic to this small treehouse.

Right: Nestling between the branches of a giant sycamore at the edge of a field, the treehouse appears to have grown along with the tree.

Computer aided designers, tree specialists, and wood craftsmen have joined together to create a new technology for treehouses, with ever greater and more intricate approaches to treetop living. This phenomenon of professional treehouse building has changed the public perception of a treehouse as a few planks of wood up a tree to being an exciting and sophisticated venture with the imagination the only limit to what is possible.

By the close of 2002 The TreeHouse Company had created over 500 treetop dwellings, becoming the biggest treehouse company in the world. With eight teams of craftsmen simultaneously working around Britain, France, Jersey, Italy, Germany, and Spain, they were creating ever larger tree complexes. The dawn of 2003 promised to bring even greater achievements, with an enormous conference treehouse being completed in a fifteenth century medieval tower near Wick, in Scotland. Construction was also set to commence on the building of the world's largest treehouse at Alnwick Castle.

Right: Support for this two-storey treehouse is provided by large knee bracers.

Below: Two simple pine trees have been transformed with the addition of a treehouse, adding a focal point to the garden.

Left: The Alnwick Garden treehouse promises to be the finest example of the treehouse builders art.

Below left: With double glazing, central heating, and fully carpeted, this comfortable treehouse has all "mod cons."

This book is a celebration of the treehouses of today. And the adventurous among you, with DIY skills, will be thrilled to follow in the footsteps of The TreeHouse Company and have the chance to build your very own treehouse with a step-by-step guide.

The crafting of this book has been an amazing journey into the lives of trees, treehouses, and their owners. Each treehouse featured in this book is distinct, with the personality of its owner and the character of its host—the tree—fused together to create a unique building.

John Harris
2003

Right: With many rope bridges and interlinking decks the Alnwick Garden treehouse project will be an exciting experience for all its visitors.

Below: The TreeHouse Company are delighted to be designers of the world's largest treehouse, being constructed in Northumberland, England.

TREEHOUSES FOR CHILDREN

Nobody ever forgets that special place where they used to play as a child. It might have been a backyard shed or a wigwam, but to you it was paradise. It was a special place to run to when things went wrong, when you had plans to make and stories to tell. Maybe you were lucky and somebody had built you a treehouse.

Opposite page: A hollowed tree trunk constructed by The TreeHouse Company makes a two-level fantasy hideaway for small children.

Right: These two boys will make use of their treehouse for many years to come.

Far right: Painted in bright colors this treehouse is welcoming and fun.

THE APPLE TREEHOUSE

Perfectly crafted from top to bottom, it is hard to spot this little treehouse among the dense foliage, unless you know just where to look.

Opposite page: A playhouse with a difference—these children can spy on approaching grown-ups through the apple-shaped peep-hole carved out of the treehouse door. The building was especially designed to be child size inside: Adults No Entry!

Even a small treehouse can present a challenge to the master craftsman. This diminutive children's playroom tucked secretively into the boughs of a thirty-year-old apple tree in an orchard belonging to an old Tudor house in Surrey, England, is a treehouse that appears deceptively simple—especially when compared to the grandiose schemes seen elsewhere in this book. But take a closer look. The apple tree that supports it is a complex host, from the main trunk grow a myriad tangled branches. As the aim of the treehouse builder is not to harm the tree in anyway, but to attempt to leave it better off that it was previously, these present a problem. Each and every one of those branches must be incorporated into the treehouse, a painstaking and lengthy task, but one that yields a great benefit. In spring, the

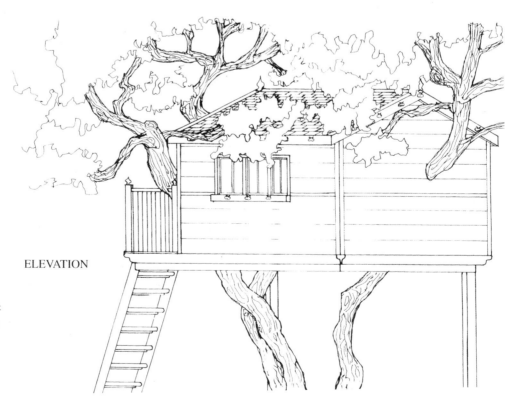

ELEVATION

Right: The original hand-drawing of the treehouse shows the care that the designer had in ensuring that no undue stress would be put on the apple tree. Instead, stilts help to prop up the building.

This page: Small is beautiful. The
TreeHouse Company's colored
impression of the finished treehouse
is almost hidden behind a blaze of
blossom in springtime. When the fall
arrives, the family can stand on the
balcony and pick apples from the
upper branches.

tree will blossom and, the interior of the house being well lit, its flowers appear there as well as on the outside branches. For a few short weeks this is a sweet-smelling place to be and as enchanting a treehouse as even the most complicated and expensive.

The owners of this charming treehouse approached The TreeHouse Company in the closing months of 1998, having read about their work in a national newspaper. The family had recently purchased a beautiful sixteenth century house, which over the years had accrued some less attractive extensions and additions. Their aim was to remove these and rebuild in sympathy with the original house. Of course, this meant that their home had been a builder's yard for some

considerable time, and not a great environment for their two young children. In recognition of this, and as a token of thanks to the children's patience and good behavior while the work was ongoing, the parents engaged the author to design and build a refuge, a place to which the children could escape, and where they would find some wonderful childhood memories. The parents' request was that this should be a space suitable for children, built to a child's dimensions, and offering secrecy away from the building and decorating work going on around them. The actual design was left to the company.

The TreeHouse Company's response was simple and traditional, the type of treehouse that will be familiar to many as the

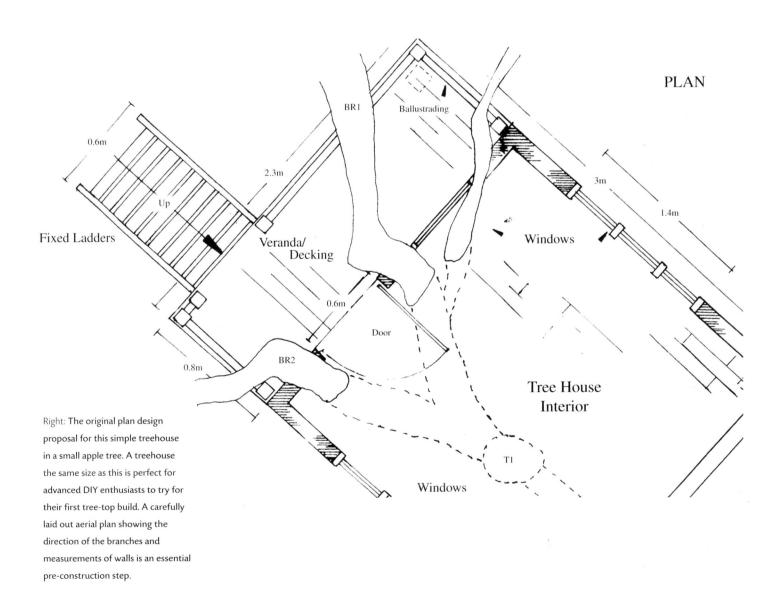

PLAN

Right: The original plan design proposal for this simple treehouse in a small apple tree. A treehouse the same size as this is perfect for advanced DIY enthusiasts to try for their first tree-top build. A carefully laid out aerial plan showing the direction of the branches and measurements of walls is an essential pre-construction step.

Left: The children had no idea that a treehouse was being built for them. A special present from their mother and father, they discovered this wonderful building sitting in their apple orchard when they returned from holidaying abroad.

epitome of what a treehouse should be, and recognizable to anyone who spent their childhood in the trees. Square, with a small veranda to the front only and two-way pitched roof, it would have windows on each side—important to the foliage within—and a central door to the front. From front to back, including the veranda, the plans showed a complete structure measuring seven feet by ten feet, with the house itself being seven feet square, a size that would be comfortably supported by the tree, and, aesthetically, would not overwhelm it.

The family approved the design immediately and work began in April 1999, taking two craftsmen a fortnight to complete; quick work considering the complexity of the job. Having surveyed the tree at the design stage and deciding the level at which the treehouse would be best situated, the first task was to install the main joists for the supporting platform, upon which 6" x ¾" flooring was laid. The basic shape of the house followed in Scandinavian pine. Real difficulty only began when it came time to construct the walls and roof. The nature of the tree dictated that each piece of wood needed to be individually, and carefully, shaped to accommodate the thirty-odd branches that pass through the treehouse, not an easy task even for the most experienced of carpenters.

However, the tree did offer reimbursement for this challenging work and a problem generally faced in bigger trees with fewer boughs was not such a trouble here. Because the apple tree has many small branches, the movement of each is less apparent, even in high winds, and consequently less allowance needed to be made though, naturally, a certain amount of space was left around each branch to allow for some shifting, as well as for the tree's growth. There were also fewer practical considerations than usually faced during the building of more elaborate treehouses. This was to be a simple place for children to play and needed no heat source or electricity.

The basic structure complete, the walls were made of log-effect tongue-and-groove timber and the door of tongue-and-groove ½" floorboards. The balustrade was completed with 1½" round dowels, and the roof of ¾" marine ply topped with French felt shingles. The treehouse was then stained in green and brown to blend with the tree, and a finishing detail was added—an apple shape cut into the door, providing an appealing touch as well as a peep-hole for the children to peer at anyone approaching. Access to the treehouse is gained by means of a double-runged ladder, easy for small hands and feet to climb and safer and more stable than a rope ladder.

Inside, the treehouse is unexpectedly airy, offering plenty of room for play, even though the children must duck under and between the branches that dominate the space. The interior has been left deliberately unfinished—this is a simple place for the children to bring their toys and games and to camp out rather than a well-appointed showpiece.

After two long—and often frustrating—weeks for the builders the treehouse was finished and awaited its young occupants. Though certainly not the grandest of structures it was perfectly suited to its task, and provides a magical space for the children who will play here for years to come. In winter it blends well with the tree, but it is in the spring, summer, and fall that it is at its best. The blossom of spring is followed by dense foliage in summer; now it is the most secretive of hideaways, hidden and protected by the leaves of the tree and, with leaves within too, feeling like a space inside the tree itself. In fall the children can stand on the veranda and pick the tree's golden fruit straight from the upper branches as the leaves turn color around them. The treehouse is perfectly built to the scale of the children, offering them a sanctuary, a place apart from the adult world.

Designer: **Leane Cairns**

Craftsmen: **Willie McCubbin (team leader), Brian Keown**

Dimensions: **7' x 10' (with veranda)**

7' x 7' (treehouse)

Materials: **Scandinavian pine (joists and structural)**

ridged softwood decking (veranda)

6" x ¾" planed timber boards (flooring inside)

Log-effect tongue-and-groove (walls)

¾" marine ply (roof)

French felt shingles

1½" round dowling (balustrade)

Wood stain

Sophie's Treehouse

True to the spirit of the oak tree, a remarkably mature competition winning design by an eleven-year-old girl.

The credit for designing this delightful treehouse goes to its owner, a young girl called Sophie. For a number of years the author has run an annual competition in conjunction with a British national newspaper. Entrants submit a drawing of their ideal treehouse and the winner has their design built for them. From the hundreds of entries in 2002 Sophie's was selected because it showed a great deal of thought in its planning and attention had obviously been paid to its surroundings. The drawing showed a treehouse that picked up the detail of its oak tree host in its design and made an effort to blend with its setting. Where other children had designed helicopter and space-ship treehouses or fantasy castles and even a Chinese pagoda, the winning design was remarkably mature, and, uniquely among all the entries, included a scale so that the judges could see the size of the structure.

Having had the competition pointed out to her by her mother Sophie sat at the kitchen table with the oak tree as her inspiration and drew a modestly sized treehouse with an acorn-shaped door, an acorn knocker, and windows shaped like oak leaves. She thought that a pointed wavy-edged roof would look

Left: Rachel de Thames and the author present Sophie with her award at the official prize giving ceremony during the Chelsea Flower Show 2002.

Right: Sophie's dream treehouse brought to life by The TreeHouse Company craftsmen. She beat hundreds of other hopefuls, who had entries ranging from space rockets to pyramids, in order to win a treehouse of her own design.

most natural, and that it should be thatched to help hide the building away in the tree. On the very top of the roof she drew an acorn and to camouflage the treehouse even more, she colored the timber walls brown to match the tree bark and the door the same shade as the leaves in summertime. A railing was added around the platform to stop her and her friends falling off, and again her theme was reflected in the carefully sketched acorn finials on the railing posts. Finishing touches were a rope bridge walkway to a deck in another tree on the opposite side of the pond, solar powered lanterns, a basket pulley, and an emergency rope ladder. Having finished the drawing Sophie posted it and promptly forgot all about it. A few months later she was most surprised to receive a telephone call telling her that the design was among the final fifteen.

Once the shortlist had been whittled down to the final three, another factor working in Sophie's favor was the setting of her treehouse. To make sure that it was actually possible to build the winner there was a site inspection of each of the last three finalists. Although the judges realized that not every entrant was lucky enough to live in as picturesque a setting as Sophie, it was difficult to ignore the fact that the sturdy oak tree on the side of a large pond surrounded by beautiful countryside was a perfect setting. With the final selection already going in Sophie's favor, it made the decision a little easier.

The first step in bringing her creation to life was to have it planned out on computer by an experienced designer. Despite the care and attention with which she had planned the treehouse, it needed to be translated into something that the craftsmen could work with and checked for safety. Surprisingly, the only feature to be removed was the walkway across the pond as it was quite an expanse to traverse and the risk of falling in was considered too great. Instead, the rope bridge would be attached to a deck in a closer tree on the same bank. When inspecting the eighty-year-old gnarled oak tree host of the main treehouse it was found that the roots were exposed on the

Right: Sophie's original drawing was praised by the author for acknowledging the tree she wanted to build in as well as her use of scale—mature concepts for someone her age. She also added solar power and rope-bridges to her design.

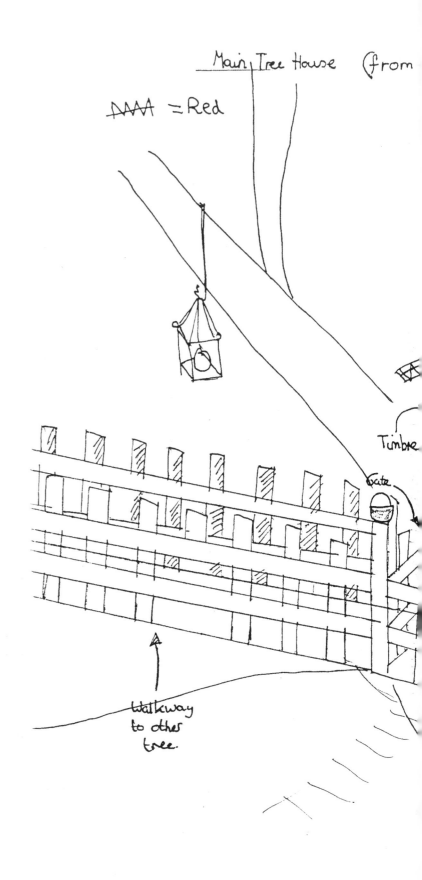

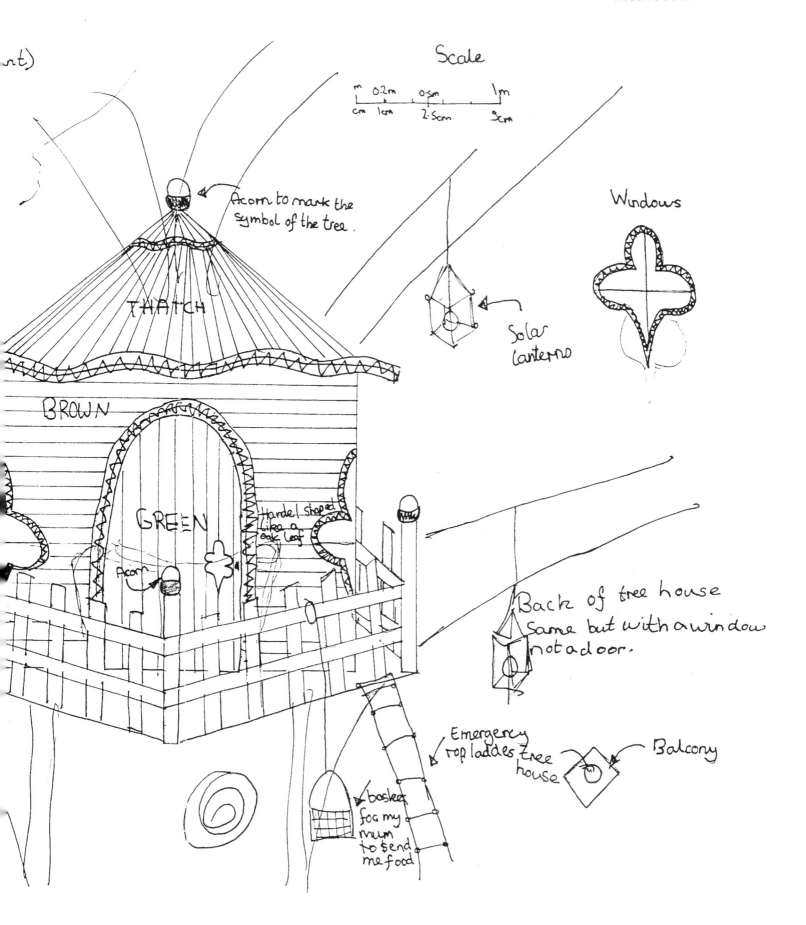

nt)

Scale

m   0.2m   0.5m   1m
cm   1cm   2.5cm   5cm

Acorn to mark the
symbol of the tree.

THATCH

Windows

Solar
lanterns

BROWN

GREEN

Handel shaped
like a
oak leaf

Acorn

Back of tree house
Same but with a window
not a door.

Emergency
rop ladder tree
house

Balcony

basket
for my
mum
to send
me food

Above: A stunning location for a treehouse. The group of oak trees used to host the tree-building overlook a small lake, where the banks are a blaze of color in springtime.

Left: Sophie's oak tree themed design incorporated even small details, such as the acorn finials that were carved onto the balustrades of her treehouse deck.

bank running down to the water and had been eroded on that side. The treehouse would have to be built to avoid putting undue stress on them. Fortunately this would actually help the tree to live longer, the weight of the new treehouse training it to the other side. In every other respect though Sophie's design was followed rigidly.

The construction took place quite quickly in order to meet a publication deadline, and took three craftsmen only two weeks. The house is built of tongue-and-groove log-effect timbers, and is lined inside, while the exterior decking and the floor inside are of hardwood. The roof is South African reed thatching, lined on the interior with ¼" marine ply. Around the base of the treehouse scalloped tongue-and-groove boarding has been added and all of the acorn detailing called for in the original design is present. Access is gained by a rope ladder to the lookout deck and a fixed double-runged ladder to the main deck.

Where other treehouses in this book have been built for younger children to tire themselves out this is a hangout for a young teenager so electricity has been run in, allowing Sophie to listen to music, and there is an oil filled radiator to keep her warm during evenings spent on homework. Sophie, who has decorated the interior with considerable taste, brought up the soft furnishings herself as well as a desk and armchair, though the boughs running through the treehouse also make a very comfortable seat for friends. The oak leaf-shaped windows offer a view out over the pond and back toward the house.

In addition to the fun of running the competition and the pleasure in giving a child the treehouse of their dreams, the author finds the competition extremely valuable in offering an insight into the minds of children, who are often the final users of their treehouses. Although only one can win the competition there are always a huge amount of excellent designs, and often the thought processes that went into them are emulated by the designers when they are planning a treehouse specifically for children.

Right top: The treehouse boasts windows shaped like oak leaves, an acorn shaped door, and thatched roof with a carved acorn perched on the top. Sophie chose the autumn brown and leafy green color wood stains to blend in with the surroundings.

Right: The treehouse has become the perfect hangout for Sophie and her friends, for picnics, ghost stories, summer water fights, and sleepovers. She says it's also the perfect place to escape from chores and hide from her parents.

Designer: **Sophie Hughes/Leane Cairns (reworking)**

Craftsmen: **Jim Wales (team leader), Brian Keown,**
   Derek Saunderson

Dimensions: **10' x 13' (with veranda)**
   10' x 10' (octagonal treehouse)

Materials: **Scandinavian pine (joists and structural)**
   Hardwood (flooring on veranda and interior)
   Log-effect tongue-and-groove (walls)
   Flat 3" cladding (interior lining)
   South African reed thatch (roof)
   2" x 1" (balustrade)
   Wood stain

A RIVERSIDE TREEHOUSE

"Dreamily he fell to considering what a nice snug dwelling-place it would make for an animal with few wants and fond of a bijou riverside residence, above flood level and remote from noise and dust."

Mole (on first seeing Rat's home) from *The Wind in the Willows*

At the bottom of this family garden stands a weeping willow tree, leaning over a fence and trailing its branches in a small river. The fence is there for safety, to stop the youngest children from wandering too close to the water, but it also obstructs the garden's best feature—its riverside situation. The solution: a treehouse with a veranda that would overlook the water below, but be a safe place for even the youngest to play. This would not be the family's first, the father had built one a few years previously for the eldest boys. It was well used and lots of fun, but eventually it broke in the wind during a winter storm. It did give the family a taste of treetop life, however, and the idea of combining such a great area for play with an idyllic veranda where adults could unwind over the cool river was too good to pass up.

Opposite page: **The Cox family** make full use of their treehouse in the summer months, when they enjoy entertaining on the veranda and watching the river flow by. The three boys like taking the rowboat out and splashing about on the water on a hot day.

Left: Painted in forget-me-not blue and seagrass colors, the treehouse blends in perfectly with its surroundings on the banks of the river, the vivid green foliage of the willow enclosing the pretty stilt-raised building within its canopy.

The author was called in and decided to build in a weeping willow over the ruins of an old summerhouse, a run-down building that had been reduced to rubble and wire over the years. The weeping willow looks like a complicated tree to build it, and, indeed, it has many branches that all need to be accommodated. It is also a very flexible tree and due to a large canopy that catches the wind it moves significantly, meaning that extra space has to be allowed around the branches, particularly when, like this treehouse, the structure is supported on stilts rather than the tree itself. It does, however, have one advantage in that before drooping its long branches in characteristic weeping willow style, its main boughs all grow in one direction—upward—which makes them easier to work with.

After the area was cleared of the summerhouse rubble, a platform was erected on the stilts. The many twisting and turning willow branches (about a dozen were incorporated into the structure) were left to grow in peace, while the building was shaped to fit the tree.

Left: "Believe me, my young friend, there is nothing—absolutely nothing—half so much worth doing as simply messing about in boats." Rat, from *The Wind in the Willows*.

A little ducking and clambering over thick branches is required to navigate the treehouse balcony, but it only adds to the fun of being up a tree.

The family's main concern was that the treehouse should not ruin the view of the garden from the main house, so the style and color of the building were of great importance, and have been executed in a charming manner. The outside of the building is extremely pretty. A simple structure with a green, felt-shingled roof sloping down toward the river, and a broad veranda running around three sides, the door-way was fitted between the main boughs of the willow tree and the walls covered with marine plywood above a dado rail at windowsill height, and tongue-and groove vertical boards below. The walls are pierced by eight normal windows and two octagonal windows, which flood the interior with light (as always the windows were fitted with polycarbonate rather than glass, for safety). The treehouse was built quite low to the ground (about five feet on the garden side with the riverside veranda about eight feet above the water) as the family want-ed to be as close to the river as possible while still in a treehouse. Access to the veranda is by a spiral staircase in the garden. Unusually for treehouse dwellers, the family chose to have it colored in bright, startling colors. Painted in seagrass, willow, and forget-me-knot blues, the treehouse echoes the colors of the summer sky and river-water, while being camouflaged by the weeping willow. To complete the look, coconut rope was wound up the blue and green staircase.

Inside, the treehouse was split into two levels, one for playing and picnicking, and the top level for use as a sleeping loft with a fixed ladder for access and a safety balustrade. While up on the bunks, the children can spy on the rest of the family from the octagonal porthole windows. The look of the interior is very different from the outside. The color scheme is just as bright, but the walls and floor are stained a rich color called Autumn Leaf, while sills and bunks are painted in bright, pepper reds. The furniture is freestanding and was brought up especially by the family for its practicality. There is electricity for light-ing, though the children prefer to use lanterns for the spooky atmosphere they create, and radiators to keep it warm in cold months. The whole treehouse is lit by spotlights outside.

A good treehouse should always provide something that could not be had by any other means. Usually this is the view coupled with the serenity of a treetop retreat. In this case however, the

Designer: **Gordon Brown**

Craftsmen: **Jim Wales** (team leader), **Brian Keown,**
Stephen Kitchen

Dimensions: 28' x 18' (with veranda)
20' x 12' (treehouse)

Materials: 8" x 2" Scandinavian pine (joists and structural)

6" diameter stilts

Non-slip ridged decking

Tongue-and groove floorboards (interior)

Marine plywood (exterior walls)

Vertical tongue-and-groove boarding (exterior walls and door)

Round felt shingles

Neoprene (collar around the trunk)

2" round posts (balustrade)

3" x 2" timber (double rung ladder to sleeping loft)

Polycarbonate windows

12" x 2" Douglas fir (spiral staircase)

Exterior paint in various shades

treehouse has opened up much more. The parents enjoy it for summer evenings on the veranda over the cooling river looking out on the meadows opposite, while for the children it means that they can enjoy the river in a controlled fashion. Since it has been built the older ones have found that they can jump from the roof into the water below, while the youngest can fish from the veranda. Underneath, the treehouse shelters a rowboat, for use of the older children, while the river is still fenced off from those it might endanger. Like Rat's home in *The Wind in the Willows* it is snug inside all year round and remote from noise and dust, the perfect place for games and relaxation.

THE ADVENTURE TREEHOUSE

Decks with dizzying views down to the ground and safe railings all the way round, connected by two rope bridges. Double-rung ladders that are easy to scramble up, a look-out deck, a zip slide, and, of course, the treehouse itself—spacious enough inside for the three children to use as a sleeping loft.

This adventure complex, with the treehouse at the center, is a child's paradise, a private playground off limits to adults (though parents have been know to sneak up on a summer evening to relax with a glass of wine). Designed and built with great attention to the surrounding environment it looks like it could have been cut from the forest that afternoon. It's also close enough to the main house for a quick dash back for drinks or food while far enough away to be hidden from grown-up eyes. But perhaps the most attractive feature of this tree is its location. The house and its grounds are upon a hill and the forested area where the treehouse is built is the highest point. From the treehouse's veranda, sheltered by an overhanging gable, the children have a view through the forest and over the village and countryside, a view that is even better from the crow's nest. At night they can look down and see the lights of the houses twinkling beneath them.

The Baker family came across The TreeHouse Company at the Chelsea Flower Show in May 2000 and immediately took to the idea of having a treehouse of their own. The gardens of their home are more formal than child friendly, being carefully planted and maintained and dotted with sculpture, but, fortunately, they also have a small, forested area to the side of the house, and this is where the children go to play. It is also an ideal location for a treehouse. Another good reason for having a treehouse was that Mrs Baker runs an interior design service and frequently has clients to visit her at home. Many have children and the treehouse would provide them with entertainment, leaving their parents and Mrs Baker free to discuss projects.

As a designer Mrs Baker participated heavily in the planning stage of the treehouse, having very specific ideas of what she wanted—a rustic and organic-looking Swiss Family Robinson structure that looked like it was a part of the forest. She wished to have it connect three old large lime trees together and "provide an exciting environment for play."

The design that she and The TreeHouse Company finally settled on was a center-piece treehouse, with a veranda, measuring fifteen feet by twelve feet and situated thirty feet from the ground. To give the children a sense of unassailability the only approaches to

Opposite page: The treehouse roof was shaped to a point to provide a place to hoist the basket pulley up and down, as well as sheltering the balcony from sudden bursts of rain.

it would be across eighteen foot rope bridges from decks in the other two trees; a large eight-sided deck with a crow's nest lookout above it in one tree, and a smaller five-sided deck in the other. The decks themselves were to be reached by rope ladders that could be pulled up after the children or by a double-rung fixed ladder. From the treehouse itself to the forest floor there is a zip slide, and there are also two swings and knotted rope for climbing.

Building in these 100-year-old trees was straightforward, taking three craftsmen just four and a half weeks. The treehouse and decks were all constructed in the boles of the trees, where growth and movement is minimal. About a millimeter of growth a year is usual for this type of mature hardwood, so enough room could easily be left around the trunks for fifteen to eighteen years

growth. Of course, no branches were removed and the tree was not damaged in any other way. The only small problem to be dealt with was that lime trees exude a sweet-smelling sap. While this would give the treehouse a wonderful fragrance it also attracts insects. However, their numbers could easily be kept down by means of screens fixed over the windows.

The basic structure and the decks were built of Scandinavian red pine, which is a good quality, durable material. The outside is covered with Scottish pine, left resolutely coarse with its bark still attached, for the "cut from the forest that afternoon" look that Mrs Baker wanted. While Scottish pine is not the best quality wood that could have been used here it does have the ability to look rough. Despite appearances however, this treehouse is built to last and, as with almost all the timber that The TreeHouse Company use, the pine was first pressure treated, with preservatives forced into the fibers of the timber. For extra protection, and color, the wood was then treated on site with wood stains, allowing the structure to blend even more with its surroundings. The roof was made of cedar shingles, again left rough, while the ropework for the bridges is rustic looking, though hiding steel cabling for extra strength and safety.

The crude look was also carried through to the interior. Here the walls were again stained in Volcanic Ash, and no soft furnishings were brought up: this is a camp, not a home away from home. Around the tree trunk, which runs through the center, The TreeHouse Company craftsmen fashioned a table, again left to look as rough as possible, and the ceiling was left unlined—looking up you can see the underside of the shingles. One touch was added by the client after the treehouse was finished—leaf stenciling on the floor, which was then protected with a coat of varnish.

Left: The ultimate in children's adventure playgrounds, with five decks, button swings, rope ladders, two basket pulleys, several rope-bridges, and a zip slide.

Right: Lime trees are wonderful hosts for any treehouse, with their bright green summer foliage and bunches of winter-time mistletoe. The height and maturity of these trees meant that they could support several platforms and rope bridges as well as the main house.

The treehouse is in constant use by the Baker children as well as their friends. On warm days, the heat can hardly penetrate the foliage and delicious fruits hang on all sides. Two baskets operated by pulleys mean that the children can hoist their favorite foods up to the treehouse in preparation for a night in the trees (there is enough room for four of them to camp out in sleeping bags). There are board games and two battery-powered lanterns, which mean they can stay up into the night and make as much noise as they want; there are no adults to complain.

Designer: **Gordon Brown/Mrs Baker**

Craftsmen: **Ronnie Butcher (team leader),**
  Peter Tudhope, George Grossart

Dimensions: **15' x 12' (with veranda)**
  9' x 12' (treehouse)

Materials: **Scandinavian red pine (joists, structural,**
  decking)
  Smooth 6" floorboards (flooring inside)
  Undressed Scottish pine (wall cladding)
  Cedar shingles (roof)
  2" round posts (balustrade)
  Wood stain

THE GOTHIC TREEHOUSE

Inspired by the architecture of chivalry and romance, this treehouse is the perfect setting for young knights and princesses.

A fantasy treehouse can be anything you want it to be. Over the last few years many eclectic treehouses have been constructed, complete with various spectacular and unexpected features, such as a jacuzzi, a crystal chandelier, a heavy oil-burning stove for treetop banquets, and even a powerful telescope has been given pride of place on its own sycamore tree observatory deck. When the author visited the country home of this client to discuss their requirements for a treehouse he received a complicated design brief for a project that would be truly original. The treehouse was to be a fusion of two cultures, two traditions, and two historically different types of architecture: not an easy thing to create

Right: The hand drawings give a good indication of what the final building will look like in its designated position. Yet as any of The TreeHouse Company craftsmen could tell you, the final finished product looks far superior.

Right and below: **This fantasy treehouse, a fusion of Gothic and Middle Eastern styles, is fully equipped with lighting and heating, and even has a sleeping loft for sleepovers with a futon bed and silk drapes.**

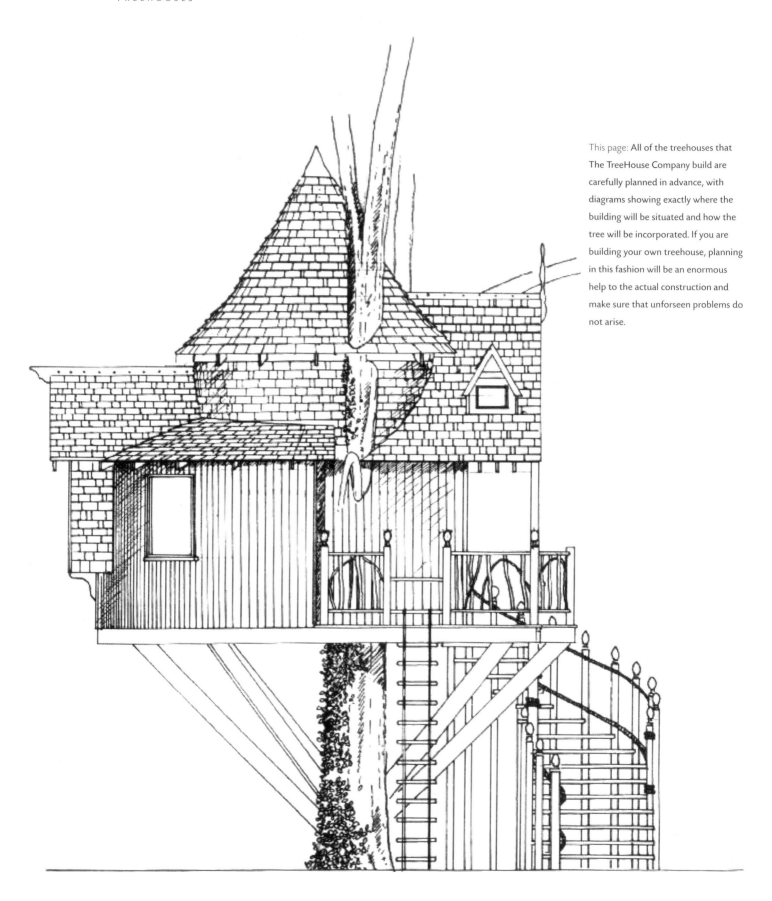

This page: All of the treehouses that The TreeHouse Company build are carefully planned in advance, with diagrams showing exactly where the building will be situated and how the tree will be incorporated. If you are building your own treehouse, planning in this fashion will be an enormous help to the actual construction and make sure that unforseen problems do not arise.

convincingly. To add to the difficulties, the sycamore trees that were proposed as the hosts for the structure were thickly grouped together. It was impossible to take the photographs that the designers usually use for building computer-aided drawings, so the final proposal had to be made using the more traditional method of watercolor sketches.

The designer looked at several types of European architecture in researching influences that could be incorporated into the brief before settling on the Gothic style as the force behind the appearance of the building. It was hoped that the use of Gothic features would provide a link to common shapes in the buildings of Islamic architecture, which traditionally uses domes, minarets, round forms, and curves with the use of regular patterns and intricate decoration, and has an organic feel that would suit treetop buildings. By combining these influences with Gothic architecture, the designer intended to create an ethereal looking structure that would look as if it had been taken from the pages of a fairy-tale, while retaining elements of Gothic grandeur. An additional advantage of taking inspiration from Gothic buildings was found in the style's preference for large windows instead of heavy walls. This

would allow the interior of the treehouse to be flooded with natural light.

The brief also called for the building to be split into two levels, with a playing and living space on the lower floor and a ladder reaching up to a sleeping loft. Here, it would be impossible to imitate the interior of Gothic buildings, with their high vaulted ceilings in great swathes of curving stone. Instead, a curved, paneled ceiling was designed to look more like a Bedouin tent, with ceilings just low enough to let adults know that it was a building intended only for children. To finish off the design a futon bed for the sleeping loft complete with silk drapes was proposed.

The estate on which this fantastic treehouse is built is of national historic interest, and a year of negotiations with Historic England had to be undertaken before permission was given for the construction of a treehouse in such a sensitive area. Early in 2002 the permit for building was granted and construction began on one of the most complicated treehouses ever to be built in Britain. Although not huge, it would take almost two months to complete.

The construction of the treehouse was difficult from the beginning, with seven huge forty-five degree knee bracers needed to

Right: A long rope bridge stretches through the sun-dappled canopy to reach a far sycamore tree which holds a triangular-shaped sun deck. The rope bridge is constructed from non-slip ridged pine slats, with metal chains to take the weight, and coconut rope wound along handrails. It is firmly bolted together to provide solid support.

Above: The double doors of the treehouse are designed in the Gothic manner to give the impression of a cathedral in the forest. The light filtering through the numerous windows makes the interior seem airy and spacious, though the small inner dimensions are perfect for children to feel as if the place is really their own.

Above: The specially made shaped window looks out from one end of the upper sleeping loft.

Above: A ship's ladder, constructed like the rest of the treehouse from cedar, is the way up to the second floor.

support the large platform in a very tight space among the trees. Once the basic red pine framework was assembled, all the remaining exterior wood had to be put in place. As the treehouse had been designed with very few flat planes, almost every piece of wood had to be individually measured and scribed to fit. The majority of the wood inside and out is cedar, used in smooth vertical boards for the walls and also shingled on the roof, turrets, and dormer windows. The outside of the building was intended to weather beautifully, with the untreated cedar turning a silvery-gray color in winter-time and altering in shade throughout the year. The cedar used inside also gives the room a lovely aroma.

The structure of the building is rather unusual; a spiral staircase leads up to a curved half-moon entrance deck with a natural wood balustrade. From here the children are able to explore by crossing a rope-bridge and scrambling down an escape rope-ladder to the forest floor. The rope bridge reaches from the deck through a jungle of bushes across to an especially sunny triangular platform and has been built with a good amount of swing and jump in it, so it is fun to run across, and doesn't simply hang static and rigid. The Gothic arched doorway to the treehouse interior also opens out onto the main deck. A curved overhang shelters the doorway from rain, while providing a secret little room on the top floor that is reached by a ladder through a trapdoor, and from where the children can spy out from the tiny windows of their "Bedouin tent."

The treehouse's focal point is a quatrefoil window high in the building—a round window composed of four equal lobes like the petals on a flower—a feature that is common to both Moorish and Gothic architecture. The red framework of the window is intended to give the effect of stained glass. On the opposite side of the treehouse a large dormer window overlooks parkland, and has a pointed arch slightly curved and softened to give it more of a Middle Eastern feel.

The designer drew inspiration for the main entrance to the treehouse from the great twelfth century cathedral of Notre Dame in Paris. The double glass doors rising to a pointed arch are a replica of the outline of Notre Dame's doors (a shape that also features prominently in formal Middle Eastern buildings). A six-sided turret, which is taken from the International Gothic style, was added to the roof design, with a further fusion of cultures being found in the small capital in the shape of an onion dome used to crown it. This is a miniature reference to the great onion shaped domes of religious temples that can be found throughout the Middle East. More architectural detailing can be seen in the ridge-beams of the frame, which extend out from the treehouse and have unusual carved curving ends.

Inside, the treehouse was also given special attention, with heating and electricity installed for year-round use. Special wall lights were crafted in metal, with shades of soft, pale leather. The lower windows were made to open out onto beautiful views of the estate while a built-in window seat also looks out into the park, and is a perfect place to sit at sunset.

The completed treehouse is a tribute to fine design and craftsmanship. Looking as though it has been lodged into the boughs for centuries, it is a place of adventure and comfort. It is in constant use through every season: in summer it is a leafy adventure playground, while in colder months it is a cozy place for games and stories. With its influences rooted in tales of romantic chivalry and the *Arabian Nights* it is hard to imagine anywhere more suited to children or more likely to spark their imaginations. Obviously, the cost for a treehouse built to this standard is high, but the money buys childhood memories for its occupants that are beyond value.

Above right: This curved balcony has a rope ladder entrance as well as a spiral staircase leading up from the ground. The balustrades were constructed only from materials found in the grounds and add to the curvaceous, organic feel of the Middle Eastern design elements.

Designer: **Gordon Brown**

Craftsmen: **Jim Wales** (team leader), **Henry Durham,**
 Gerry Sollit

Dimensions: **28′ x 15′** (with veranda)
 18′ x 15′ (treehouse)

Materials: **Red pine** (joists and structural)
 Hardwood (flooring on veranda and interior)
 Cedar (walls, interior and exterior)
 Cedar shingles (roof)
 Natural ash branches (balustrade)

A Castle in the Sky

*Knights, wizards, fire-breathing dragons, and fair maidens spring to life in the
imaginations of the lucky children who play in this Camelot treehouse.*

It is difficult to imagine a more exciting environment for young children than this. Inspired
by myth, legend, and fairy tales, the treehouse is a private castle, where over forty children
can make believe in towers, battlements, and feasting halls. Wars are waged in its ramparts
and princes win the hearts of fair maidens held captive in the turrets. There are few parents
who would go to such lengths to provide a setting so redolent of chivalry and romance, but
the result of their generosity is truly awe-inspiring and will leave an indelible and magical
mark on the memories of their fortunate children.

The only constraint on the building of this fantasy treehouse was the quality of the
trees themselves. The perfect position for the complex was in a place that offered less-than-
perfect trees; a copse of sycamore saplings none of which was more than twelve years old,
but situated a couple of hundred yards from the house on the opposite side of a walled garden and completely hidden from view, offering complete privacy for the children and the
freedom to believe that they are in an enchanted kingdom far away from home. So long as
the treehouse could be built here the parents were happy for The TreeHouse Company to
be as adventurous as necessary with the design.

The only option open to the designers was to create a treehouse that would support itself, but be flexible enough to accommodate the trees as they grew; a case of the
trees growing to fit the treehouse rather than the other way around. While this is unusual it
offers a great benefit to the trees in that the structure will give them support as they grow.
The treehouse would have to be built on stilts around the trees, and would need professional attention every two years to make sure that neither the trees or the castle were
suffering. With an otherwise unlimited palette the designer went to town on a medieval-
looking castle complete with turrets, towers, and thin windows for archers to repel
attackers. There would be four different levels in all, with four rooms as well as spiral staircases inside the turrets to the battlements. The roofing would be flat, offering even more

Opposite page: **This impressive fantasy
castle looks as if it has sprung straight
from the pages of a storybook. Built
on stilts, with tree branches running
through the interior, it has four round
rooms, a large veranda, and three flat
look-out turrets. If this isn't enough
for aspiring knights to enjoy, there are
also rope-bridges leading to other
tree-decks.**

Left: Hidden away in the woods at the
bottom of the garden the large
treehouse castle blends into the trees.

room for adventure, with the ramparts making sure that no-one could fall off. The children would even be able to fox their friends by making use of a hidden trapdoor in the topmost turret or another secret door between two of the rooms, neither of which would be easily found unless the children wished to let special friends in on the mystery. The only entrance to the castle itself would be through a special gatehouse, which would give the sense of entering a real castle and also lend itself to games of attack and defence.

All of this would be supported on stilts six inches thick. Great care was taken in placing these, as no damage could be inflicted on the roots of the trees, so all digging was by hand and the holes were filled in if there was any danger. After the joists of the platform had been raised onto the stilts, the flooring was laid. It was decided to use hardwood for all of the outside decking and interior flooring, as while it is more expensive it is also more durable and less liable to expansion or contraction. With the platform complete the castle's framework was erected and covered with vertical tongue-and-groove board (the verticality helping to create the impression of a tall and mighty castle) with half-round log-effect timbers used for battlements and towers. With the doors and windows positioned the exterior was stained in Autumn Leaf and Light Oak. The turrets were topped with green shingle tiles and lead capping.

Inside the castle, all of the rooms and turrets were lined with vertical tongue-and-groove board and black galvanized fixtures and fitting, such as door bracers in Gothic style, were added. Curved

Left: Suspended above the ground on stilts the treehouse castle seems to float in the air. Designed with great attention to safety and the well-being of the trees that grow through it, with proper attention the fantastic structure will continue to give pleasure to children for generations to come.

benches, designed to fold down into beds, were constructed around the walls and extra storage space was also built in. For safety, it was decide to bring electricity in to run the authentic-looking light fittings, rather than have torches and oil lanterns.

The project took a team leader and three craftsmen only five weeks to complete, and is a testament to flexible and imaginative design. Although this treehouse does not have the strong presence of the trees themselves in the same way that other projects in this book do, it shows that with the application of a little creativity almost any healthy tree can be adapted to a treehouse. As the trees in this amazing castle grow more mature they will become more and more a part of the building, and with care and maintenance the treehouse will provide a fantasy setting for generations to come. In the meantime, its present occupants are the rightful rulers of their own magical kingdom, a land of limitless possibilities and endless fun.

Designer: Leane Cairns

Craftsmen: Jim Wales (team leader),

Paul Templeman, Derek Ross, Derek Sanderson

Dimensions: 32' x 27' (with veranda),

24' x 24' (treehouse)

Materials: 8" x 2" Scandinavian pine (joists and

structural)

Hardwood non-slip ridged decking

Hardwood floorboards (interior)

Vertical tongue-and-groove boarding (exterior

covering, doors, and interior lining)

Half-round log-effect (exterior turret walls and

doors and battlements)

French felt shingles

Polycarbonate windows

Wood stain

Galvanized fixtures and fittings

Above: The gatehouse provides the only way into the treehouse, adding to the feeling that this is a real castle.

A TREEHOUSE PLAY COMPLEX

Four decks and a true house in the trees, with beds for nights in the leafy canopy. The children can stay up there for days on end.

This lofty playground was conceived when Martin Rositer, a grandfather of fourteen children, moved into a Victorian house. High up in a 250-year-old cluster of oak, pine, and sycamore trees was an old homemade platform, which had obviously been well used by the children of the house's previous owners. Having a stock of suitable wood already, Martin initially decided that a couple of decks linked by a rope bridge would be just the place for his legion of grandchildren to enjoy themselves, and the author was contacted. The initial brief was to build the platforms as "a really rough and tumble area where there would be loads of active play and the children could enjoy using their imagination," however the building seemed to have a life of its own. By the time that the design was complete the planned complex spanned five trees, with four decks linked by long rope bridges, and a two-storey treehouse that would sleep eight children comfortably. The treehouse would also eventually make Martin something of a celebrity—TV companies and the press from as far away as Australia and Los Angeles covered the story of the Englishman who had built such an amazing treehouse for his grandchildren.

The stand of trees which was to host the buildings was unusual in being almost a wild wood, with both hard and softwoods growing in untamed profusion. A survey found that all were good strong trees, however, and a number were mapped out as hosts for the building work. The finished complex was to span two oaks and two pines for the platforms and a sycamore for the house itself. The only difficulty that the selected trees presented to the designers was that the different species would move in various ways. For example the pines are tall and thin to reach the sunlight, and as a result they catch more wind and have a greater sway than the other trees. Fortunately, this problem was, in fact, very simple to solve. As the design progressed no fixed connection was planned between any two of the structures. Access from deck to deck was to be by rope bridge only. More slack than usual could be built into these bridges, ensuring that the trees could sway independently of each

Opposite page: The main treehouse is constructed in a sycamore tree with a trunk running straight through the center.

Right: Two verandas allow for relaxation and contemplation, while inside an upper level loft has a hatch to climb up higher to another small veranda.

other without causing any damage to the treehouse, the decks, or themselves.

Having grown and grown the final design showed a small square deck that was reached from the only fixed bridge in the plan, which started on a bank opposite, meaning there would be no problem with movement. Beneath this deck was a button swing and from it would run the longest rope bridge to another square deck, which could also be accessed by a rope ladder. The rope bridge from here would provide access to the veranda of the house itself, beneath which is another swing. From the treehouse a rope bridge crosses to a larger octagonal deck, which can also be gained by a fixed ladder that is easier for the smaller children to climb. The last rope bridge leads to a square deck that is roofed in the same style as the treehouse and is also accessed by a fixed ladder.

The design was approved at once by the client (the treehouse was wanted as quickly as possible so that the children could start enjoying it) and construction took four people only six weeks. As is usual the basic structure is of pressure treated softwood (Scandinavian pine), which was treated again onsite, but due to the size of the build-

ing the joists in this case were a larger than normal 9" x 3". Machined decking was used on all the decks as it is both attractive and provides traction for slippery soles in wet weather. Balustrades around the decks are simple 1.5" round posts with 5" posts at the corners. Again, safety was a primary concern and these are fairly high to prevent smaller children falling out, though low enough for most to see over. The connecting rope bridges are all woven from manila, a natural fiber, which contributes to the organic feel of the complex, and the high tensile steel chains that provide support are disguised by broad treads.

The treehouse itself is a rustic brown color called African Walnut, with waney-edged horizontal boarding on the outside. This is boarding that has not been squared off after being cut from the log, so it has a much more organic appearance. In this case it makes the treehouse look like a real woodcutter's cottage. The roof is of cedar shingles, which are lightweight and weather beautifully. Inside, running water and electricity have been installed for cooking and cleaning and to run the fridge that stores picnic supplies. There is a simple sink with cold running water in the kitchen area along with a microwave oven. Electric heating means that it is cosy all year round. The bottom floor

Left: This combination of treehouse and decks was built for the whole family to enjoy, at least when the children let the adults get a look in.

is an open space of a height that will comfortably accommodate adults with the old sycamore that supports the structure running through it, while the bedroom upstairs is much more child sized. The latter is reached through a hatch by ladder and has a quaint dormer window and a small veranda that is built like a poop deck and even has a ship's wheel for sailing the swaying treehouse through the forest canopy. There is a large bed built in, which sleeps three children, as well as bunk beds and space on the floor for further camping mattresses. All of the interior walls are lined with tongue-and-groove vertical boarding, which gives a "cabin" feel, and the doors and units are of the same wood and style, which could be described as "neatly rustic." The décor is very basic as ease of cleaning was a priority. Walls have been left varnished, while the spaces between the tree and the treehouse have been sealed with rope, making the building completely watertight, and even insect proof.

Martin Rositer's grandchildren must be among the luckiest in the world. This extraordinary treetop complex gives them an adventure playground that looks like it could have come straight from a film set. Like most of the owners of the children's treehouses in this book, this generous grandfather will admit to taking advantage of the treehouse when the opportunity presents itself, but with so many children in the family, all of whom adore their treehouse, his chances to do so in peace and quiet are few.

Designer: Mark Waterfield

Craftsmen: Jim Wales (team leader), Paul Templeman (team leader), David Gregory, Jenny Dutton

Dimensions: 20' x 16' (with veranda)
14' x 12' (treehouse)

Materials: 9" x 3" Scandinavian pine (joists and structural)

Non-slip ridged decking

Tongue-and-groove floorboards (flooring inside)

Waney-edged horizontal boarding (exterior walls)

Vertical tongue-and-groove boarding (interior walls)

Cedar shingles

1½" round dowling with 5" corner posts (balustrade)

Manila rope and high tensile steel chain (rope bridges)

Wood stain

THE KINDERGARTEN TREEHOUSE

A combination of classroom and fairytale, an imaginative space and magical place for children to grow and learn in.

Opposite page: Special toys and games are reserved for the older nursery children when they spend time in the treehouse. The walls, free of lining board, provide little shelves for storage and decoration.

Below: These shutters, exquisitely carved with love hearts, were requested by The TreeHouse Company's client to give a real gingerbread house feel to the building.

The client's brief for this treehouse was to emphasize the word "special." The owner of a private kindergarten catering for about thirty children wanted something that would give her school a competitive edge, something that other kindergartens didn't have, as well as providing something wonderful for the children, a magical place that would not be used all of the time but occasionally as a treat. Her initial thoughts were to convert the garden or a small patch of beech trees into an adventure playground area, but having read about The TreeHouse Company in the national press she finally decided on a treehouse as it could be used even in cold months. Once she had made the decision she formed a very particular idea of what she wanted, and even drew her own, well executed, sketches and plans of the fantasy classroom. It was to be in a Swiss chalet style, reminiscent of a Hans Christian Anderson story, with feature windows wherever possible and finished to a very high standard.

After the initial survey, during which it was decided to build around a beech of about fifty years old, the sketches were taken back to the office and worked into a design that could be accommodated around the tree. Two big classrooms were needed, and the beech would not be able to support the weight of a building of this size, so the treehouse needed to be supported on stilts. The tree was young and would grow comparatively quickly and this also needed to be taken into account. Added to the fact that building on stilts meant that the treehouse would not be able to move with the tree, more room than usual would have to be left around the trunk so that the tree would not damage itself or the building. The design was discussed and refined over some time with the client until she was happy with the proposed building down to the smallest detail. Safety was, of course, her paramount concern. An additional obstacle was that a

Above: The children think that their treehouse is wonderful. It is designed to be the perfect height for nursery school children to run around inside, and for adults to sit and help with the songs, games, and storytelling.

commercial building of this size needed planning permission from local authorities before construction could begin.

It was to be raised only a little way from the ground (just over five feet), and shaped like the letter "L" with a cute bay window. With a mixture of vertical and horizontal wooden slats rising to a triangular tiled roof it would resemble the alpine chalet the client wanted. The windows were all to be arched, with wooden shutters, window boxes, and heart-shaped cut-outs providing "fairytale" touches. A little gate would lead up the wide stairs to a small veranda where the children could leave their boots in wet weather.

With the design approved (the final plan was significantly bigger than had been planned initially) work began in September 2001, six months after the first survey, with three craftsmen working on the project under a team leader.

Before the platform that would support the treehouse could be raised the stilts had to be placed. In order to protect the tree, holes were dug by hand and if any roots were encountered the hole was

Left: The bay window was an essential requirement in the treehouse design, letting lots of light flood into the interior of the playroom.

filled again and digging begun elsewhere. It is important to note that this method of construction also produces a "rain shadow:" that is the treehouse shields the ground beneath the tree from the rain, so the tree needs to be carefully watered for twenty-four hours twice a year in spring and fall.

It must have been very exciting for the children to see their treehouse playrooms being built, watching the craftsmen cut wood and hoist up walls and doors into the air, and walk around in harnesses on the roof while it was being tiled. Despite its size the work proceeded like any other treehouse, the platform being made first (with big 10" x 3" joists topped with the floorboards) followed by the framework. The exterior of the building was completed with half-round log-effect covering, while inside the floor, walls, and ceiling were insulated before being lined. The roof was finished with cedar shingles and a safety balustrade added around the veranda and the fixed staircase leading up to the treehouse. The latter was given high and low handrails so that children of all ages would have a safe hold. The door, window frames (fitted low so that the children can see out), and shutters were fashioned from hardwood and carved with love-hearts. Around the ground below the treehouse a fence was built with a lockable gate ensuring that children can only gain access under supervision. After its completion, electricity was installed and two corner stoves fitted to warm the rooms.

Inside the wooden chalet the children had to be protected from splinters, so after every surface was stained a light oak color before being highly polished. The floor was stenciled with autumnal leaves and lacquered until it gleamed. All the windows were given locks so that small hands cannot open them.

The décor of the two rooms is very much as any other in a kindergarten. The client decided against integral features and fittings in order to make the space as versatile as possible; furniture can be moved around to make room to make a stage, for a comfortable storytelling area, or for a more traditional classroom. The walls are lined with the children's paintings.

The final result must be one of the most unique and imaginative classrooms in the world. With every safety precaution taken, the children have a secure, but very unusual place to learn and play, and one that they cannot wait to get into. The first children to be brought up here were in awe and wonder, and this that hasn't worn off with familiarity. The client has found that the children are always particularly absorbed in their playing when they are up here; there must be something about treehouses, a natural environment perhaps, that gives children better concentration and makes them more relaxed and happy. This really is a "special" place for children, and, as with treehouse office spaces for adults, it seems to inspire those who work and play within. Surely there should be more schools built like this.

Designer: **Leane Cairns**

Craftsmen: **Ronnie Butcher (team leader),**
     Colin McCauley, Brian Keown, Chris Wilson

Dimensions: **44' x 36' (with veranda)**
     40' x 36' (treehouse)

Materials: **10" x 3" Scandinavian pine (joists and**
     structural)

Non-slip ridged decking

Tongue-and-groove floorboards (interior)

Half-round log-effect (exterior walls)

Cedar shingles

Neoprene (collar around the trunk)

2" x 2" timber (balustrade)

Polycarbonate windows

Wood stain

A TREEHOUSE IN FRANCE

A delightfully eccentric building of muted greens and browns perfectly camouflaged in the treetop canopy.

In the heart of the Maures Mountains, bordering the gulf of St.Tropez, is a secret hideaway hidden among a stand of gnarled spruce pine trees that have had a hard life in a landscape that never sees much rain. The treehouse is a gift from a father to his children, and looks out on some of the most spectacular scenery in France. In one direction an old, ruined castle, destroyed by Cardinal Richelieu, rises over the village, while below, Provence is sprawled in the sun. From the other side of the treehouse you can look down to the beach and the endless blue of the Atlantic Ocean. At night the view is even more enchanting. From the heights of the treehouse the lights of Provence can be seen twinkling for miles.

Like many of the parents planning a treehouse for their children, the owner of this amazing structure had a hideaway of his own as a child and remembered how important it had been to him while growing up to have a place where adults would rarely venture, a place of adventures where the imagination was the only limit to his fun. Wanting to give his own children something of the same experience his instructions to the author called for a safe treehouse not too far off the ground, close enough to the house yet hidden from view, with lots of entrances and interesting accessories to make it a really entertaining adventure play area. Quality was also a requirement, as well as the necessity for a building that would reflect the local environment and fit organically within the beautiful landscape of the grounds and the surrounding countryside.

It was decided to use a cluster of fir trees at the bottom of the house's vineyard and create a really grand affair. With the proximity of the ocean a nautical theme was employed in the design; porthole windows look out toward the beach while on the top level is a "poop deck." The main house would be built with two of the trees running through and have three roof levels, a large covered porch, dormer windows, and a raised veranda. Access would be by spiral staircase, and a rope bridge would lead from the

Opposite page: **The TreeHouse Company** use computer aided design to give their prospective clients a realistic depiction of the finished treehouse. A photograph of the site and any trees to be used is merged with the specifications of the customer, right down to the smallest details of color and material used for the roofing and balustrades.

Above: A stunning site for any prospective treehouse, overlooking mandarin and palm trees to an ancient ruined castle in the distance. The family add their grapes from the vineyard to the local co-operative to produce a fruity red wine.

veranda to a deck in a third tree. If you were to walk around this treehouse you would find it taking on a quite different appearance from each angle. The design was deliberately muddled and eccentric, a crazy toy-town building that would look as if it had been assembled gradually with new add-ons of verandas and dormer windows.

The TreeHouse Company's design was accepted immediately and a team of craftsmen was dispatched with their tools. The building materials were all to be sourced locally to help the house fit within the local scenery and it was planned to make extensive use of the local pine, which has a closer grain than that found in the north of Europe, the result of slower growth due to less rain.

The finished treehouse relies upon the generosity of the trees—it is perfectly balanced and held in place by the tree boughs, with no need for any additional support. All joists were bolted to the dead heartwood of the tree so that the tree growth will extend along the bolt rather than pushing it outward, weakening the structure. To allow the two trees incorporated in the main house to move independently of each other sliding brackets were used so in the breeze the whole house sways gently, but there is never a danger of the trees damaging the structure or themselves. The treehouse was covered on the exterior and fully lined inside with the local pine, which was stained in greens with light brown highlights outside to help the treehouse blend with the pines. The veranda was made safe with a trellis balustrade while the rope bridge to the secondary deck was constructed of steel cables disguised with manila ropework. A novel problem for the craftsmen was the discovery of a vicious breed of spider in the trees, which had quite a bite. These are now prevented from climbing by coating the base of the tree with a substance that dissuades them.

Inside, the pine lining was bleached almost white, and, along with the double glazed windows, this helps to keep the interior cool. The summer heat can be fairly intense here, so electricity was installed in part to run a fridge that could keep the children supplied with cold drinks without the need for running back to the main house. The room below can seat six adults (if they are allowed up) in comfort while above the sleeping loft can accommodate four children in two double, built-in futons. The craftsmen also shaped a table around the trunk of the tree, and built bookshelves and benches with storage space beneath.

As will be mentioned more than once in this book, a classic treehouse will give the owner something that nothing else can. This treehouse, already in a stunning setting, opened up vistas of the sea and surrounding countryside that cannot be seen from anywhere else in the house's grounds. Since it was completed the treehouse has become a focal point for the whole family; while the children play aloft the adults entertain below, though it is often difficult to keep guests on the ground. Up in

Right: A TreeHouse Company watercolor gave the prospective owner an idea of the "feel" of the treehouse.

Left: The treehouse owner wanted the building to be as hidden as possible among the copse of evergreens. The green and brown staining as well as a green felt tile roof, contribute to this effect. Here you can also see the nautical theme, influenced by nearby St. Tropez, with the ship's wheel for the children to play with up on the balcony.

the trees the children eat on the upper veranda, and take turns playing with the ship's wheel. When the breeze moves the treehouse it is easy for them to imagine that they are steering a ship down toward the blue ocean. However, it is when there are no adults around that this treehouse achieves its true purpose. With its swings, verandas, rope bridges, deck, and sleeping loft, it affords the children a sense of privacy and is a place where they can explore their independence in safety, and let their imaginations take them to magical childhood places without hindrance.

Designer: **Gordon Brown**

Craftsmen: **Jim Wales** (team leader), **Martin Wood, Derek Ross, Peter Beetschen**

Dimensions: **24' x 24'** (with veranda)

24' x 20' (treehouse)

Materials: **8" x 3" Scandinavian pine** (joists and structural)

Ridged decking

Smooth floorboards (interior)

Local pine (interior lining, exterior walls, and integral furniture)

French felt shingles (green)

Neoprene (collar around the trunk)

Red pine (trellis balustrade)

Wood stain

Above: **Constructed out of pale pine, the interior is great for children of all ages to use, with a corner table wrapped around the trunk and carved benches to match, plus a ladder to climb up through a trapdoor to the next level.**

TREEHOUSES FOR ADULTS

Whether designed for luxury and comfort, or made to become a part of nature, a treehouse offers a place away from normal life. You can choose to use it as an office, as a place to gather with friends, as a simple retreat—anything you can imagine.

Below: Suspended over a pond containing koi carp this treehouse is designed to suit the Japanese-style garden.

Above: High in the canopy, this adult treehouse is a place of refuge and retreat.

Right: The author's favorite treehouse. At the edge of a formal garden hidden within a great Scots Pine is a beautiful small treehouse.

THE RED OFFICE TREEHOUSE

There is something quite unique about working so close to nature, in a place where the wind and rain can be heard, where water runs down leaves and soaks into the bark, and you can almost feel the sap rising.

Over the last few years many people have found the treehouse to be an amazingly versatile space. From tiny serene reading rooms to adventure complexes, almost any kind of building can be lodged in the trees. But in one area in particular treehouses are growing in popularity—as small home offices. For those who now rely on technology rather than a large staff, the treehouse offers an amazing work space; distanced from everyday distractions it can easily be built to provide heat, light, and comfort, and with the addition of a telephone line or two it can also provide all the telecommunications necessary for a modern business. Of course, almost any space can be adapted to the same purpose, but the people who are now working from a treehouse have invariably found that there is something about the atmosphere that increases their productivity while making them feel more relaxed.

The owner of this treehouse had found that working from home is not an ideal situation when there are young children around. It was hard for him to ignore the demands of little ones who could not understand that "Daddy is working." In order to provide himself with a secluded place to work undisturbed, he chose to construct an office in the extensive gardens of his home, at a distance from the house. Originally, he considered building a prefabricated log cabin, but while visiting The TreeHouse Company's exhibit at the Chelsea Flower Show in May of 2002, he was amazed to find that it would cost a relatively small amount more to have his own bespoke building raised in a tree.

As the chairman of a homeopathic company with a great interest in the protection and nurture of plant-life, it made sense for the client to ask the author to construct him a home office. A member of both the Arboricultural Association and the International Society of Arboriculture, The TreeHouse Company is wholly dedicated to proper tree care.

Opposite page: **A bold and vivid design statement, the pillarbox red treehouse looks impressive when framed against a blue springtime sky.**

Left: The superb sycamore tree that
will play host to the treehouse office.

The TreeHouse Company craftsmen do not damage the trees used in
the construction in any way, and take great care to preserve the long
life of each tree host. Timber used in this house was selected Canadian
and Scandinavian redwood, purchased from recognized forestry companies who exceed all replanting requirements and have
well-managed forests.

As well as being concerned about the environmental impact of
the office structure, the client also felt it was important that the
treehouse be a tailor-made dwelling that would reflect the personality
of its owner, and his career in alternative medicine. This office treehouse was to be an appropriate working environment for the head of
a company that deals with the healing power of plants, herbs, and
flowers. Many people find that being in a treehouse is an excellent way
of re-establishing a connection with the earth, inhabiting a place not
walled in by concrete, but made from natural resources. There is a creative power that can be tapped into up in the trees, which can inspire
ideas or help solve seemingly difficult problems.

When it came to the design of the treehouse, the client wanted something that, while fulfilling all the sophisticated needs of a
modern office, would demonstrate the idea of a treehouse as a magical place, quite different from a normal house. Inspiration was taken
from E.H. Shepard's illustrations in the stories of Winnie-the-Pooh and
the American Colonial Style. The treehouse would have clapperboard
cladding painted bright pillarbox red, with French windows folding out
onto a veranda, and a balcony running from the back to the front of
the building. Inside, a wood-burning stove fitted with its own chimney
would provide warmth during the winter. This would make reinforce-
ment beams necessary to support a stone base and back, which the
stove would need in order to protect the surrounding timbers from
being scorched or weakened. The client also wished to take advantage
of the stunning views of the surrounding hills by having a large
window where his desk would sit.

The construction was rather unusual. The platform space allo-
cated for the treehouse was quite large (20" x 12"), and in order to
support the treehouse, enormous knee bracers would have to be
used. These would have touched the ground and been far too bulky,
so a more elegant solution was found. Support for the treehouse was
split between between smaller knee bracers and ½" steel cables that

Right: Balancing work life and home
life. The TreeHouse Company's client
was considering building a prefabricated log cabin in his garden until
he came across the idea of treehouse
living. Now he can get work done with
few distractions apart from the
fabulous view.

Left: With its nautical windows and wood-burning stove puffing out smoke through the chimney, the treehouse has an air of yesteryear charm, combined with high-tech office facilities such as internet access, a fax machine, and laptop computer.

Left: The corner window lets lots of daylight into the interior, creating a harmonious environment close to nature; an ideal office for one of Britain's leading homeopathists.

were fixed to extended platform joists, and suspended from the top of the sycamore tree. These were attached to the tree by arboreal harnesses with a twenty ton breaking strain.

The finished treehouse is a red building of ten foot by sixteen foot, with a veranda around two sides and looks like something out of a fable with the wood smoke rising from the chimney. Two small privet trees guard the bottom of a two-way staircase. Inside, the walls are covered with horizontal lining boards painted cream and the ceiling is scattered with small white ceiling lights. It is a modern space with a laid-back atmosphere. There are three windows, each of which is unique—a nautical round window is wrapped in coconut rope, and there is also an arched window and a panoramic corner window in front of the desk, as requested by the client. The exterior's red and white theme is echoed in all the furnishings, with red shelves, filing cabinets, chairs, a doormat, and even a small red kettle. The carpet is pale brown, covered with a red and white rug. A comfortable red and white striped chair sits near the double veranda doors.

The office is equipped with everything you would expect, including a telephone and fax machine, lap-top computer, and broadband Internet connection. It also has a fridge and a sink for daytime lunches or evening entertaining. The sycamore tree seems huge inside the treehouse, but it does not dominate, framed as it is against one wall. The office is a sun-trap on warm days, but during colder months the black iron wood-burning stove provides all the warmth necessary as well as a wonderful aroma.

Designer: **Gordon Brown**

Craftsmen: **Stuart Carmichael (team leader),**

Derek Saunderson, George Grossart,

Ronnie Butcher

Dimensions: **20' x 12' (with veranda)**

10' x 16' (treehouse)

Materials: **9" x 3" Scandinavian redwood (joists and**

structural)

Knee bracers

4" x 1" ribbed softwood (decking)

5" x ½" tongue-and-groove boards (interior

floorboards)

5" x ¾" clapperboard (exterior walls)

Horizontal tongue-and-groove boarding (interior

walls)

Canadian cedar shingles

Neoprene (collar around the trunk)

2" x 2" (balustrade)

2" x 3" timber (window frames)

Double glazed windows

12" x 2" timber (staircase)

Exterior paint in red and white

A FESTIVE TREEHOUSE

Covered in wisteria in summer, and with a veranda perfect for catching fall sunlight,

it is in winter that this cosy treehouse is at its best.

Traditionally, most treehouses are simple places that only come to life during the warmer months. However, if you have the vision—as this family did—to create a space big enough for entertaining in style and install heating and electricity, with a little imagination you open up your treehouse to a whole new world of possibilities. For example, the treehouse on these pages has hosted a full Christmas dinner for ten, in great comfort and in an atmosphere redolent of the ancient pagan festival of Yuletide. What better place could there be for a midwinter feast than in a beautifully crafted and decorated wooden lodge high in the trees? The brief called for a large treehouse, suitable for entertaining, with an integral dining table. This was to be very much a place for adults, an unusual and informal space where the hosts and their guests could really let their hair down. Nevertheless, the family did not want their children to miss out on all the fun, so it was suggested that a playdeck with swings and slides should be linked to the main treehouse.

The tree selected to hold this retreat was a 150-year-old ash, the only tree in the garden that would be able to hold the weight of a treehouse this size within its branches. Ash trees are known for their powerful roots and ability to withstand great pressure, so, as it was perfectly healthy, the tree would allow the designer to work on a grand scale. At only a few yards from the main house it was also perfectly situated for food to be prepared there and brought up to the treehouse, which would save the cost of installing a rudimentary kitchen.

The treehouse was designed to an octagonal form twenty feet in diameter and just under nine feet high. The shape would give an organic feel to the tree-space, and it would lend itself to a veranda running around six sides, which would catch the sunshine at any time of the day and provide wonderful views. The trunk of the ash tree was to be the central spoke of the room around which everything would be built in a circular fashion. Access would be by spiral staircase, wide enough to carry up a tray safely, while

Opposite page: **The grand old ash tree, decorated for a Christmas party, is a wonderful central feature of the room.**

Above: The treehouse has been transformed into a really magical space. Dozens of candles, lanterns, and a candelabra make the interior twinkle with a soft honey glow. The dark window and interior wall mirror reflect the candlelight. Up through the skylight the stars can be seen.

the play area was to join onto the main treehouse by a fixed ladder, with lots of fun accessories such as a scramble net, slide, monkey bars, and a clubhouse. The intended use of the treehouse called for electric light and a source of heat, and, for the latter, it was decided that a log-effect gas fire would be an efficient means of heating a relatively large space while maintaining the rustic charm of the room.

Held up by 8" x 2" joists and covered with three-inch tongue-and-groove boarding inside and out the treehouse was finished with a large double door entry and a red felt shingle roof, with skylights fitted so that the occupants could look up into the stars

treehouse becomes a enchanting place to bring guests. It is impossible not to relax up here, away from all sense of normal everyday life. At Christmastime, with ivy and decorations hung from the ash tree that runs through the center it is a quite magical space, with a unique atmosphere—a blend of traditional Christmas past with a touch of something older and wilder.

at night. Like all the author's treehouses it is well blended with its environment and is a very attractive garden feature in its own right. It is the interior though, that is of particular interest, and shows what can be achieved with a little creativity. Once The TreeHouse Company team had left, the client went to work to add a few features that really give character to the treehouse. The inside walls of the room were stained green to merge with the feel of the tree, an old Victorian cabinet was found in a second hand shop, and an art glass window panel was bought from a salvage yard and restored. A candelabra was suspended from the ceiling over the integral table, and an enormous mirror hung on one wall, so that the inside of the treehouse seems to expand, reflecting space and light.

With the wood-burner effect fire blazing and the space lit by the candelabra, candles, and discrete low voltage spotlights the

Designer: **Gordon Brown**

Craftsmen: **Willie McCubbin (team leader),**

Jim Wales, Brian Keown

Dimensions: 24' diameter (with veranda)

20' diameter (treehouse)

Materials: 8" x 3" Scandinavian pine (joists and

structural)

Ridged decking

Tongue-and-groove floorboards (interior)

3" tongue-and-groove (interior lining and

exterior walls)

Red felt shingles

Neoprene (collar around the trunk)

10" x 2" ash timber (spiral staircase)

2" ash timber (balustrade)

Double skin polycarbonate windows

Wood stain

A TREEHOUSE FOR DINING

Illuminated by discreet lighting, warmed by a log-burning stove, and decorated with antique furniture and paintings, this dining room treehouse is cozy and inviting.

On arriving at the home of the client to discuss their needs for a treehouse, the author found the occupants had gone, leaving this note pinned to the front door:

> *"To The Treehouse Man*
> *We would like a substantial house with veranda,*
> *to sleep two adults, two children, and to house*
> *a small Aga oven. We'd like it for children's use,*
> *but the odd dinner for ourselves!*
> *Thanks."*

> The Hillcoat Family

In those few sweet lines, was the most demanding request the author had been given in the short history of the company. It would be only the eighth treehouse undertaken, but one that would lead to much bigger and greater things. Featured heavily in the national press it went beyond anything that had gone before it and would bring new projects pouring in. This was unknown at the time, of course, and, reading the note again, the author was simply concerned with how these seemingly straightforward requests could be met.

The first thing to do was to look for a host suitable for a treehouse on this scale. There was really only one candidate—a venerable and gnarled old willow near to the garden boundary. It was large enough to accommodate the biggest treehouse the author had designed so far, but had one, or, more accurately, twenty-seven significant drawbacks. While there was a natural space for a considerable building at the crown of the tree, the twenty-seven branches rising around it would pose serious difficulties, not least of which was could a structure possibly be stable that was pierced by so many boughs? Nevertheless, it was a challenge; if this treehouse could be built then it would set the standard for the future, so

Opposite page: **The completed treehouse adds rather than detracts to the beauty of this grand willow tree.**

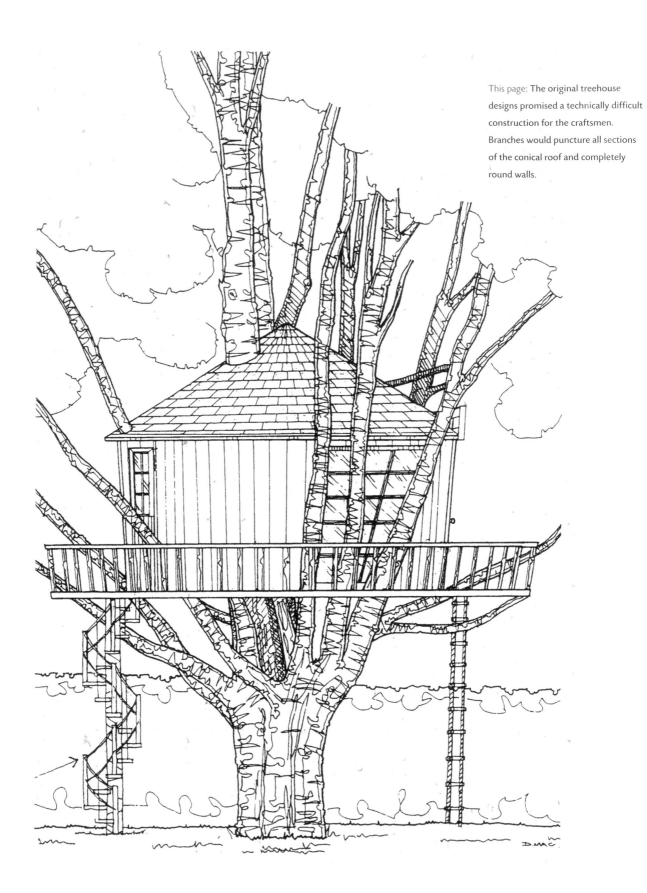

This page: The original treehouse
designs promised a technically difficult
construction for the craftsmen.
Branches would puncture all sections
of the conical roof and completely
round walls.

Right: Once the deck is completed it becomes much easier to start on the complex task of constructing the walls around so many different branches.

the author began taking measurements of all the branches, how thick each was and in what position it was growing. This job alone took two hours.

With the initial designs drawn up, the clients were revisited. The family was modestly pleased with the circular treehouse surrounded by a veranda, but as they discussed the concept further and explained that they were both restaurateurs by trade, it began to dawn that what they really wanted was even bigger than had first been realized. A fridge. A freezer. Wine-racks. Low-voltage lightning, hot and cold taps, and, most importantly, a dining-room table suspended between the branches of the tree. Back to the drawing board.

The next design was approved immediately, with construction to begin within a month. As feared the branches were a problem from day one; laying the floor of the circular platform was like solving a complicated jigsaw puzzle and even finding a foothold in the labyrinthine tree was difficult. However, the platform began to take shape slowly. Two other problems needed to be addressed though; willow is a very flexible wood so the Douglas fir timber had to be fitted to the tree with specialist metal brackets that would hold it to the tree on sliders. In this way, when high winds whipped around the huge boughs, causing them to move in unpredictable directions, they would not tear the treehouse apart. The same principle would later be applied to the "floating" dining-room table. Although attached to the inner trunks in three places, the sliding mechanism allows the table to stay still while the branches of the tree sway in the wind. The last problem in laying the platform was that one corner of the tree did not provide sufficient support. However, this was easy to solve in that a spiral staircase could be installed here around a central pole fashioned from a trimmed tree trunk that could also act as a supporting stilt.

With the platform complete, reinforced with 10" x 3" joists where the Aga cooker would later be installed, and the flooring down, work proceeded to the walls. Here, blueprints failed the craftsmen, and work progressed intuitively, with the builders incorporating the tree trunks into the walls and fitting windows shaped between the

Above: Fully fitted with heating, electricity, and cooking facilities, the interior of the treehouse is perfect for entertaining. A simple lunch becomes something more special when sharing food at the heart of a tree.

branches. Despite the complexity not one single branch or limb was removed from the tree, even the smallest twig had to be fitted through the wall or the roof.

The finished treehouse is a simple circular design that has since become something of a TreeHouse Company trademark, with the walls covered inside and out with a dark brown stained tongue-and-groove vertical boarding and surrounded by a relatively wide veranda with a simple balustrade. The roof is shingled and also stained dark brown. However, it is on the inside that this won-

Right: From a distance, the treehouse looks like a medieval roundhouse with its vertical log covering.

derful dining room in the sky is different to its predecessors. Again, the walls are lined with vertical tongue-and-groove boarding, while the roof has been left open to that you can see the supporting joists and the underside of the shingles. This doesn't help insulate the room, but it is attractive and the Aga cooker and a wood-burning stove more than compensate for the loss of heat. Low voltage lighting and tasteful paintings create a warm ambiance that is complemented by the

Designer: **John Harris**

Craftsmen: **John Harris (team leader),**

    Willie McCubbin, Jim Wales

Dimensions: **32' diameter (with veranda)**

    28' diameter (treehouse)

Materials: **Douglas fir in various sizes (joists and**

    structural)

    Ribbed decking

    Smooth floorboards (interior)

    Vertical tongue-and-groove boarding (interior

    lining, exterior walls)

    Canadian cedar shingles

    Neoprene (collars around the boughs)

    2" round dowling (balustrade)

    Hardwood doors

    Polycarbonate windows

    8' trimmed tree trunk (supporting stilt)

    12" x 2" Douglas fir (spiral staircase)

    Large shaped piece of oak (dining table)

    Wood stain

eighteenth century French cast-iron chairs around the large central dining table, which was specially carved from oak and varnished in satin. The treehouse also boasts a copper fitted sink with hot and cold running water and a skylight fitted above, as well as chunky pine fitted units in the kitchen area, a well-stocked wine rack, and windows shaped to follow the boughs of the tree.

What seemed an enormous task at the time has since become almost routine for the author, but this is still a landmark treehouse by any standard. Simple, but elegant, and in perfect harmony with its host, the structure looks as though it is a part of the tree. Luxuriously appointed, but warm and cozy, it is a room that encourages relaxation, making it an unbeatable place to entertain.

THE SYCAMORE TREEHOUSE

An enormous dome-shaped sycamore holds a treehouse for the whole family. Used for dining, entertaining, sleepovers, and just generally relaxing it is a warm den in winter and a cool sanctuary in summer.

Commissioned secretly, this treehouse was built while a husband was away on a business trip. The couple had discussed the project many times over a couple of years, but he was less enthusiastic than his wife, not realizing the benefits that the treehouse would bring. His wife's subterfuge paid off. The treehouse is now in constant use by the whole family, with its original opponent now its most ardent advocate.

The family had originally asked the author to do a site visit to discuss the possibility of a treehouse for their teenage sons, during which he found a huge sycamore of about 200 years of age in the garden. It was the perfect tree to support a substantial treehouse that could provide enough room for everyone to use in a variety of ways. Overlooking a tennis court and with views out to sea it would be the ideal place for the parents to entertain on summer evenings as well as providing a hangout for the boys where they wouldn't disturb anyone. A design was submitted soon after, showing a spacious round building in The TreeHouse Company's signature style, totally supported by the expansive tree and pierced in a number of places by its spreading boughs. A balcony would run all the way around the building, with three enormous limbs to duck under and one that you had to step over. A set of double doors would open into the room. The whole family loved the design, but it was deemed by the man of the house to be an unnecessary extravagance, and so the wrangling began. Two years later his wife decided to put an end to the discussions and simply go ahead without her husband's approval, at a time when he would not be around to protest.

The tree lent itself perfectly to a treehouse. Low in the trunk it split into thick and sturdy boughs that, with the addition of knee bracers, provided a solid support for the platform. The treehouse would take shape at the visual center of the tree, giving a sense of

Opposite page: In full summer foliage, the giant sycamore plays host to tennis suppers and sleepovers. With the doors flung open to catch a hint of cool sea breeze, the treehouse gives the family a perfect outdoor living space for entertaining their friends and family.

Left: The spiral staircase had to be constructed with some mighty uprights to support each step— it's a long way up from the ground to the treehouse platform, but once at the top, the sea view makes the climb worth while.

balance and proportion. The size and age of the branches also meant that they were easily incorporated into the structure, with minimal space needing to be left for future growth.

Once the platform had been raised and floored and the frame assembled, the outside of the building was covered in vertical log timber, and stained with country oaks and autumn browns so that it would blend in with the tree rather than draw attention to itself. During the summer it would be almost hidden under the leaves. The cone-shaped roof was covered with marine plyboard for waterproofing and finished with cedar shingles. A huge spiral staircase was hidden away at the back of the building so that from the house it looks as though the treehouse is simply floating off the ground. As an extra feature, a platform was fixed onto a nearby beech tree from where thrill-seekers could descend to the ground on a zip slide (aerial runway).

Inside the walls and ceiling were fully insulated and the former lined with vertical tongue-and-groove boarding, while the ceiling was fashioned from a beautiful redwood to look like the spokes of a wheel. Rope was wound around the base of each branch on the interior floor, and spiraled above on the ceiling. With windows and doors fitted the treehouse was nearly finished.

The client had grand plans for the interior look of the treehouse, first asking an electrician to extend a cable to the structure, giving it its own electricity supply, thus enabling her to install heating and lights. A kitchen galley was then set up with microwave, baby belling, and a kettle. The TreeHouse Company supplied two oak benches and an oak table to form a dining area and a television and video went against one wall, with shelves full of movies and games. The floor was varnished then laid over with seagrass mats, and fold-down futons with soft covers were brought in to be used as chairs during the day and beds at night. An outside light was fixed onto the exterior of the treehouse, and lanterns and candles brought inside. Mirrors, lamps, bird paintings, and butterfly prints were arranged, making for a homely, cozy den among the branches.

On windy days the whole building moves and sways, making huge creaking noises; just as you might expect if you were sailing on a ship in high seas. The treehouse has been a success for the whole family, not least for the man who opposed it for so long. The teenagers use it as a hangout that also offers sleeping room for friends who might come over for a night of movies, while the parents bring friends up for meals or to watch tennis being played on the court below. For a little additional expense the insulation and heating have created a room that can be, and is, used the entire year round. With a hammock often suspended between the interior branches it is a relaxed place with all the other benefits of a good quality treehouse—great views, peace and quiet, and the feeling of well-being that comes from days and nights spent so close to a living tree. Moving gently in the breeze up here with the shady foliage rustling gently, it is easy to see why the family spend so much time in their treehouse retreat.

Right: A chill-out zone and camp, the treehouse is fully fitted with heating and electricity so that it can be used all year round. It even has its own kitchen galley, dining-table, and comfortable sofa chairs for guests to slouch on.

Right, below: The teenagers escape from the house to watch television. In strong winds, the treehouse creaks and sways, like a ship in high seas.

Designer: **Gordon Brown**

Craftsmen: **Willie McCubbin** (team leader), **Colin McCawley, Jenny Dutton, Alan Crindle**

Dimensions: 32' diameter (with veranda)

    28' diameter (treehouse)

Materials: 10" x 2" Scandinavian pine (joists and

    structural)

    Ridged, non-slip decking

    1" thick tongue-and-groove floorboards (interior)

    Half-round log-effect (exterior walls)

    3" tongue-and-groove (interior lining)

    Redwood timber (interior ceiling)

    Marine plyboard

    Cedar shingles

    Neoprene (collar around the trunk)

    12" x 2" Douglas fir (spiral staircase)

    2" round (balustrade)

    Double glazed windows (toughened)

    Wood stain

THE GREEN TREEHOUSE

"What is that extraordinary looking building in your garden!"

Above: The arched door has a leaded top section that matches the windows and, along with the scalloped facia board, adds to the "look" of the treehouse.

Above is the first reaction of many guests who come to visit this family in their home. This is a treehouse built not only for enjoyment, but also as an unusual garden feature. Right in the middle of the rear lawn it makes a very attractive focal point as well as being a great place to relax on a warm day, and perfectly serves its primary purpose as a folly: you can see the treehouse from every room in the back of the house with particularly good views being found through the large windows of the lounge where the family spend most of their time. Designed to lend an element of fantasy to the garden, and drawing inspiration from the past, as you wander across the carefully maintained rolling lawn, past the clipped topiary, you could almost believe that there are fairies at the bottom of this quintessentially English garden.

The owners visited the Chelsea Flower Show of 2001 and fell in love with The TreeHouse Company's stained glass window treehouse. With two fir trees in the middle of their own lawn that would be perfect for a treehouse, the family did not take long in commissioning a design that would make use of the firs, trusting the look and feel of the building completely to The TreeHouse Company's designers. With the first design instantly accepted, work began in February 2002, the family being keen to use the treehouse in the spring and summer.

The trees in which it is built presented few problems for the design and building of the treehouse. With the oldest of the pair being around thirty-years-old they are both very simple and straight with no difficult forks or twisted boughs to deal with. The only real consideration was that the younger of the two has a more slender trunk than its neighbor, meaning that in winds it will move more dramatically. To address this the platform mounted on this tree is fitted with slider brackets, allowing the two trees to move independently without causing any stress to the structures they support. From start to finish work on the treehouse took three craftsmen three weeks to complete.

Opposite page: The large veranda is reached by way of a winding staircase with manila rope handrails.

Above: The two Scots pine trees on the
rear lawn that will be used to support
the treehouse.

Above: A hand drawing shows the
building at design stage. It will be an
attractive treehouse with a large
veranda linking the two trees.

The bright green treehouse, while unmissable, is at the same time unobtrusive—softy curved and covered in cedar shingles, sitting straddled between two tall fir trees. Supported by forty-five degree knee bracers the treehouse itself is two-thirds round with the last third missing, making an unusual and pretty shape. A veranda, which is finished with tree branch balustrades, leads to a low deck in the second tree where a staircase, worked through with coconut rope, spirals upward. Pine needles and fir cones from the host trees litter the deck, and the fresh pine smell up here is wonderful. The wooden walls of the treehouse feature an arched Gothic window, with leaded glass, and a small curved door leads into a tiny room. The top half of the treehouse

is of flat pine boarding, with cedar shingles below, under a dado rail. Also roofed in cedar shingles and stained in Autumn Leaf, the building is reminiscent of a Hansel *&* Gretel cottage. Fitted with electricity it is floodlit inside and out, so the family can stay up here all night and to make sure that even in the dark the treehouse can be seen from the main house.

Inside, the tree trunk is framed against the wooden walls and leaks fragrant amber sap gently. The interior has been left plain, suiting its purpose as a folly rather than a room that will be in constant use. Children might sit in here of an evening and play games, but the adults prefer to relax out on the veranda, so there is little decoration and the

Right: The completed treehouse is finished in green above the Canadian cedar shingles that match the roof.

treehouse has not been fitted with the features that can be seen in other projects elsewhere in this book.

It is mainly used on sunny days, when the adults can set up chairs and tables and eat lunch up on the deck, watching the squirrels running up and down the fir trees. The children like to play on the staircase with a football or run in and out the treehouse with their friends. But it is at night that it comes into its own. Floodlit against a background of shrubs and bushes it is a perfect backdrop to candlelit dinners with friends. As it was designed as an architectural feature, even on wintry days and nights when it would be unthinkable to use it the treehouse continues to give pleasure to the owners and their guests, looking postcard beautiful at any time of the year, but particularly when it and the firs are covered with frost and snow.

Designer: **John Harris**

Craftsmen: **Jim Wales (team leader), Gerry Sollit, Henry Durham**

Dimensions: **12′ x 18′ (with veranda)**

12′ x 8′ (treehouse)

10′ x 8′ (second deck)

Materials: **Scandinavian pine (joists and structural)**

4″ x 2″ cedar boards (flooring on veranda and interior)

Flat pine boarding/cedar shinles (walls)

Cedar shingles (roof)

Undressed larch branches (balustrade)

Wood stain

A TREEHOUSE STUDY

A private den built as an out-of-the-way working space, this small office is very much a part of its surroundings. Simple and uncluttered it is perfectly suited to quiet reflection and peaceful study.

Above: **A retreat where reading a report becomes a pleasure. Finding time to contemplate tomorrow's challenges and making decisions somehow seems easier.**

The professor who owns this charming little treehouse approached The TreeHouse Company for a room to act as a home office in the grounds of his millhouse home. A simple place to read and write in seclusion, it needed to be a building that would blend with the millhouse and its six acre Capability Brown designed garden. A little hut, raised on stilts, had previously been built beside an old copper beech next to an old red pump in the garden, and this was to be replaced with something finer, more suited to its purpose. The designer took inspiration from a very special building nearby: a delightful listed boathouse with intricate old woodwork situated at the side of a ten acre lake. And with such lovely views all around the estate, The TreeHouse Company decided to base the treehouse design around a feature dormer window rising to a pointed crest. Shaped horizontally, the window would give a panoramic view of the lake, framed by the numerous branches of the beech tree. Within, the designer planned a fitted desk and window seat, both of which would take advantage of the view.

Building work was hampered by the profusion of branches that needed to be incorporated into the structure, but the design partially compensated for this, with the treehouse being built around only the less complicated side of the tree, supported by seven bracers. To ensure that the look would be simple and organic, the builders used cedar for the interior and exterior boarding in an inverted "V" pattern similar to the woodwork of the boathouse. The decking and roof shingles were also cedar and the wood was left unstained throughout. As mentioned elsewhere, cedar weathers beautifully and

naturally, taking on different hues at different times of the year. It also has its own protective oil that has the added benefit of smelling lovely, making the interior of the treehouse a wonderfully fragrant place. Access to the little study would be via a wooden two-way staircase leading to a veranda that would be just the right size for the professor to sit and read or reflect on a summer day.

The finished treehouse is perfectly suited to its use. At six feet by ten feet internally it is just big enough to house one person in comfort. The tree trunk is framed against the interior and exterior walls, with foliage hiding the building in the summer and fall. With the addition of electricity for heating and lighting, and simple décor—a desk, an easy chair, and a few ornaments—it serves the professor as an inspiring place to read and reflect, a perfect retreat for him to lose himself in his work and one where there is no fear of his being disturbed.

Designer: **Gordon Brown**

Craftsmen: **Iain Carmichael (team leader),**
  Darren Stuart, Stephen Kitchen

Dimensions: **9' x 10' (with veranda)**
  6' x 10' (treehouse)

Materials: **8" x 2" red pine (joists and structural)**
  Cedar decking
  Cedar floorboards (interior)
  Cedar shingles (roof and exterior walls)
  Vertical tongue-and-groove boarding in cedar
    (interior and exterior lining)
  Neoprene (collars around the trunk)
  2" x 2" timber (balustrade)
  Mortice and tennon traditional door
  3" x 2" cedar timber (window frames)
  Polycarbonate windows
  10" x 2" red pine (spiral staircase)

THE OAK TREE OFFICE

It's hard to get stressed when you are working in the trees.

The owner of this treehouse would be the first to admit that he has a youthful approach to life. His philosophy is "Why grow up too much when you can introduce a little fun to every part of your life, including work? Just because you have to work, it doesn't mean you can't keep that wonderful child-like attitude to life." Where better to preserve such an outlook than a treehouse? Forget commuting, noisy offices, and the hard grind; however heavy the workload is, it is virtually impossible to get tense when there are oak boughs running through the room. But if it does get too much at times, you can take a few moments out in the hammock below.

This treehouse started out as a throwaway comment from a friend, who mentioned that a 300-year-old oak at the bottom of the client's garden needed a treehouse. With the client looking at the time for a place to work in peace and quiet, the seed of an idea quickly blossomed. A local firm was engaged to build the treehouse and had already ordered timber when the client saw an article about The TreeHouse Company and stopped the work immediately. This was exactly what he had been looking for; experienced professionals with the imagination to make his dream treehouse become a reality.

What he had in mind was part Colonial Style cottage, part chattel house in Barbados, with a flavor, too, of the main house—an old converted barn. It would need to be heated, and have electricity and stairs suitable for two dogs—the client's constant companions—to run up and down easily. The response was a design very close to the finished treehouse, with only an air conditioning duct being removed later for aesthetic reasons. Built about ten feet from the ground and with the trunk of the tree at its center, the treehouse would measure a comfortable twelve feet square, enough room for both the client and a secretary to work in. A wide, six foot veranda would run along one side with posts connecting the balustrade to the overhanging eaves of the roof, a characteristic of the Colonial Style. The dogs would be able to climb the spiral staircase easily. It was a design that

Opposite page: A place for creative inspiration—the home office taken to the treetops. The oak tree proved a perfect host for this square, chocolate-colored, shuttered building. During holidays the hammock is perfect for a sunlit rest in the garden.

Left: A covered veranda and a wine basket pulley was added for after-work relaxation.

suited the client perfectly, and only a couple of weeks later The TreeHouse Company's craftsmen arrived to begin work.

The oak was a perfect tree to build in. Old, immense, and enormously strong, it would support a building of this size without any trouble at all, hardly even noticing the work going on in its boughs. Nevertheless, with the veranda being so wide, additional support was given at two corners by four-inch diameter stilts, one of which was incorporated into the spiral staircase. The opposite corners of the house were propped with knee bracers. The decking on the veranda was made from ridged softwood, which The TreeHouse Company favors as it prevents feet slipping in wet weather. The balustrade was made from 3" x 2" shaped timber, with longer posts reaching up at intervals as if to support the extended roof that shades the veranda from sun and shelters it from rain. To harmonize with the main house and to carry the Caribbean theme, the external covering was completed in horizontal cedar weather-

board (known as clapperboard), which was stained in Jacobean Walnut, a very dark brown that matches the color of the house. The joists were stained in Light Oak as was the staircase. Window frames, the working shutters, balustrade, and the fascia covering the end of the roof beams were all painted white.

Inside, the flooring had been made (at the stage when the treehouse was just a platform) from tongue-and-groove boarding, which is easy to work with, particularly when, like this, the room is a simple square shape. An oak tree of this age will not grow very quickly, so minimal room needed to be left around the trunk or branches when it came to lining the walls, again with tongue-and-groove boards. The craftsmen also fitted a desk from the main trunk for the client's secretary. His own desk is an old freestanding rolltop with a leather captain's chair.

The décor is eclectic and reflects the personality of the tree-house's owner. There is Indian furniture, and African masks adorn the walls and the tree. A pair of proud-looking carved giraffes do not look out of place alongside a rocket ship lava lamp, vintage racing posters, and a CD rack filled with great albums from every era, from Bob Dylan to *Trainspotting*. Among all this are Winnie-the-Pooh pictures, a stuffed teddy bear, fairy lights wrapped around the tree-trunk and toy tin aircraft. There is a feeling that the treehouse is part office, part playroom, which makes for an exciting and fun work environment. With heat, light, and all the IT hardware necessary for a modern businessman to function, it is also is warm, comfortable, and functional.

Who wouldn't choose to work in the trees given the opportunity? The lucky people who are able to leave behind the bedlam of an office full of people in favor of a treehouse have found more benefits than they imagined. For example, when this treehouse was being planned and designed, the owner was so intent on getting the

Above: The interior of the treehouse is furnished with objects brought back from around the world.

Designer: **Gordon Brown**

Craftsmen: **Jim Wales (team leader), Brian Keown, Peter Beetschen, Paul Templeman**

Dimensions: 12' x 18' feet (with veranda)

12' x 12' feet (treehouse)

Materials: 8" x 3" Scandinavian pine (joists and structural)

Non-slip ridged decking

Tongue-and groove floorboards (interior)

Tongue-and-groove lining board (interior lining)

Horizontal weatherboard (exterior walls)

Canadian cedar shingles

12" x 2" Douglas fir (spiral staircase)

Neoprene (collar around the trunk)

3" x 2" shaped timber (balustrade)

Polycarbonate windows

Wood stain

White exterior paint

look of the treehouse right that he didn't think about the view. Once the platform was in place the he was surprised to find panoramic views out over the rolling hills and woods of the surrounding countryside. Then there is the unique feeling that comes from just being in a treehouse. As mentioned many times in this book it is rare today to be constantly in such close contact with nature, and it can affect people in surprising ways. Those who work in a treehouse report that they feel more relaxed, yet more able to concentrate, and that they are inspired to greater creativity than before. Surely this is the ideal working environment; perhaps everyone should work in the branches of a tree.

A Secret Hideaway

A half hour hike from the nearest road, following animal tracks, takes you to this rustic treehouse hidden at the heart of nature.

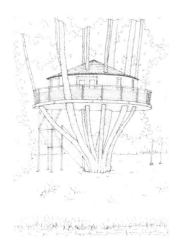

Above: The original drawing shows the treehouse supported high between the nine main boughs of a giant ash tree, with a veranda running all around the main house. It is reached by a "dog legged" staircase.

Hidden deep in the middle of a wood up in a 200-year-old ash tree is a secret hideaway miles from civilization. Built overlooking a small lake, this treehouse is situated in a remote part of one of the only remaining hardwood forests in south-west Britain. It is held in the tree, twenty-six feet from the ground, perfectly camouflaged in woody hues of brown. From its veranda you can watch deer drinking from the lake below, and all manner of birds perch in the branches to keep you company. The owners wanted a place they could go to where they would be right in the middle of nature. This is not a sophisticated lounge-style treehouse, but a rustic retreat, though more luxurious than any mountain bothy, and can be reached only by hiking through the forest with food, camping gear, and sleeping bags.

The design was very much dictated by the tree itself. Twenty-six feet up to ensure the best possible view, and to make sure that the forest's animal life would not be able to smell a human presence, the surveyor mapped a cross-section of the spreading branches. The resulting design was based around a thirty foot diameter circular platform with a veranda all the way around. Inspiration for the look of the treehouse itself was drawn from African huts.

When it was built, the craftsmen had to transport all the building materials by four-wheel drive through the fields and park half a mile from the lake. Every tool, piece of wood, and each bolt had to be carried by hand along the tiny woodland trails to reach the clearing where the ash tree stands. Once the construction began, great attention was paid to the sur-roundings, with craftsmen making sure that the forest was disturbed as little as possible and paying particular attention to the disposal of all trash. The result is worth every effort. With its cedar shingle roof and log-effect covering surrounded by a split log criss-cross balustrade it perfectly complements its host tree. Against other treehouses in this book it appears somewhat unfinished, but this is a planned roughness. For example the eaves of the roof have been left open, and other gaps are unsealed. This means that the wildlife can come right into the treehouse, and escape easily—it is not uncommon to find squirrels sitting on the big integral table. The built-in storage space, however, has been fitted with locks to keep curious creatures out. Around two of the walls are plain benches.

Left: The completed treehouse is suspended above the lake, hidden in the deep foliage of the forest canopy. When the deer come down to the water line to drink, the raised vantage point makes an ideal viewing platform.

With no electricity the owners spend the evenings talking and watching the forest activities by candlelight, completely lost in the wood, far away from any vestige of modern life. If any rambler should stumble across the treehouse the bottom of the spiral staircase is gated and locked, but so perfectly is the treehouse hidden, particularly in the leafy summer months, that they could walk directly beneath and never realize what was above them.

Designer: John Harris

Craftsmen: Willie McCubbin (team leader), John Harris, Brian Keown, Jim Wales

Dimensions: 30' diameter (with veranda)
26' feet diameter (treehouse)

Materials: 9" x 3" Scandinavian pine (joists and structural)
Ribbed softwood decking
Tongue-and groove floorboards (interior)

Log-effect, vertical tongue-and-groove boarding (external walls and interior lining)
Cedar shingles
Neoprene (collar around the trunk)
Split log (balustrade)
12" x 2" Douglas fir (staircase)
Polycarbonate windows
Wood stain (interior only)

THE AFRICAN TREEHOUSE

This luxurious and unusual treehouse is a combination of play area, conservatory, retreat, and dining room, with an African theme that gives it an unusual and attractive look.

Some of the most exciting treehouses constructed in recent years have been those inspired by far-flung lands and other cultures. Although there is no such thing as a traditional treehouse, there are many familiar images from storybooks depicting tree dwellings such as those of Winnie-the-Pooh or The Swiss Family Robinson. These pictures tend to influence the way in which treehouses are designed. Yet while there will always be a place for tiny fairy-tale tree-buildings, more and more people are discovering that treehouse design can also be innovative and experimental. Global architecture offers much that can be incorporated into the design elements and construction materials of treehouses, and these exotic influences can produce truly unique structures. This recently constructed treehouse is one such building.

The family had, for several years, been keen to install a play area for their two children, and were considering purchasing a permanent wooden climbing frame. However, when they saw an article about The TreeHouse Company their plans changed immediately. Having had a love affair with Africa for many years, they were well acquainted with the reed-thatched buildings that are seen throughout the continent. Round houses with balconies around the perimeter, they provide cool shade in the blistering heat of the day. After the decision had been made to construct a treehouse it was a natural step to take inspiration for the design from the African buildings they had admired so much on their travels. The family also requested that their treehouse be as high in the air as possible, so that there would be plenty of space for a play area underneath. The African treehouse was to be a garden retreat for relaxation, but big enough to use as both living room and dining-area, where they could hold dinner parties.

The treehouse is doubly unusual as it is set within a group of silver birch trees. Birches have shallow root systems and are not suitable for supporting large structures. In this case, the designer was careful that absolutely no weight would be put on the trees at all,

Left: The interior is decorated to add light and space to the living and dining area. Natural wood furnishings and white orchids complete the look, with the added marvel of silver birch branches blooming inside the treehouse.

Left: The inner branches are great fun for the children to climb on and there is also a fireman's pole through the living-room floor when they want to leave the adults behind and use their adventure playground below.

instead using stilts to hold up the platform of the treehouse, merely giving the impression that the building is supported by the silver birches. Because of the sheer height and scale of the work, the owners had to apply for planning permission before construction could begin, but this was fairly easily obtained from the local authorities.

Once they were able to start, The TreeHouse Company craftsmen were meticulous in their work, making sure that none of the trees were harmed in any way, and incorporating every tiny branch into the design rather than simply removing them to make an easier job of the building of the walls and roof. A rope handled spiral staircase was installed at one end of the veranda, and a fixed ladder at the other end. Inside the treehouse there is also a fireman's pole, which can be accessed through a hatch, giving the children a fun way to get down to the play area. The laying of the reed-thatched roof was quite difficult. The family were keen for the building to look as authentic as possible and the houses found in Africa have reeds hanging so low over the edge of the roof that they can be seen from the inside of the building. This is not an easy look to recreate on a European treehouse!

The finished building has a whole host of play accessories for the children beneath it—a button swing, see-saw, knotted rope, monkey bars, and cargo net. The ground has a soft bed of wood chips so there is always an easy landing. An attractive building from the outside, the interior is stunning, and one of the most luxurious spaces that The TreeHouse Company have ever created. The owners have decorated thoughtfully and tastefully and maximized its comfort. The room was given water, heating, and electricity for year-round use, with a lock on the door and an Internet connection so that it can be used as an office from time to time. It is painted white, which offsets the bark on the silver birches perfectly, and there is a cozy sofa, as well as paintings, lamps, pots of dried heather, orchids, candles, and yellow roses. A local craftsman has furnished the room with a huge table and four high-back chairs made from reclaimed driftwood, and the local blacksmith has created curtain rails that look like elongated twigs. The interior branches still burst into leaf in spring and summertime, which is an amazing sight and one that gives the family a wonderful connection to the trees. The sound system is connected to speakers out on the deck so that guests can enjoy listening to music and drinking coffee while sitting on the balcony chairs. The lighting scheme has also been taken

into consideration, with diffused lights held in place by pottery tiles inside, and subtle uplights on the roof and leading across the lawn. It is a most welcoming place on a dark evening. The owners are even growing clematis up the support posts of the treehouse to give it a more natural look. In the summer when the garden foliage is in full bloom, the treehouse will be completely hidden from view.

Since its completion in the summer of 2001, the treehouse has played host to many parties, both for adults and children. As one of the most spectacular and luxurious treehouses that has ever been constructed in Britain, it is fair to say that the treehouse has attracted a lot of attention. Even Disney called and asked if they could use the interior to film a program about Africa.

Designer: **Gordon Brown**

Craftsmen: **Brian Keown (team leader),**
Paul Templeman, Derek Ross

Dimensions: **26' x 24' (with veranda)**
22' x 24' (treehouse)

Materials: **9" x 3" Scandinavian pine (joists and**
structural)

Ribbed hardwood decking

5" x ¾" floorboards (interior)

Tongue-and-groove log-effect (exterior
walls)

Tongue-and-groove board (interior walls)

Reed thatch

Neoprene (collar around the trunk)

2" round dowling (balustrade)

2" x 2" hardwood timber (window frames)

Carved door frame in cedar

Double glazed windows (toughened)

Wood stain

White exterior paint

TREEHOUSE EXTRAVAGANCE

A lakeside setting with views across a beautifully cultivated garden would make any treehouse here a gem. Add an unlimited budget, and the result is a special place indeed.

Opposite page: The formal lake in the foreground gives an interesting reflection of the treehouse.

Built in a stunning historic garden, this treehouse was designed for the most discerning of clients to the highest possible standards, and shows just what is possible if you have the vision—and the budget—to take a treehouse to the limits. When The TreeHouse Company was first approached in the spring of 2002 it soon became apparent that this would become one of the most magnificent treehouses that the company had ever built. The first thing in its favor would be the setting—a garden laid out centuries ago and carefully maintained ever since. All the trees here are of specimen quality, meaning that they were carefully cultivated from parents that were known to be excellent examples of their species—particularly beautiful, strong, and healthy. Secondly, the client knew exactly what he wanted: a treehouse of the highest possible caliber.

The brief called for a big round structure, which would be used for quite formal entertainment. Seating eight for dinner it was to have a full kitchen with hot and cold running water, a stove, and a fridge/freezer, as well as a fully functioning bathroom. To the rear

Right: Canadian cedar shingles were used on the lower part of the walls as well as the roof, breaking up the impression of the building's size.

Above: **Construction of the treehouse was not made any simpler by the dense vegetation under the tree, which meant long searches for dropped tools.**

would be a balcony and to the front a veranda. The tree selected as host was a 140-year-old multi-stemmed ash set back from, but overlooking, the lake. A grand old tree, and well maintained during its long life, it would support the building about fifteen feet up, affording a view from the veranda over the water to the Georgian main house.

The author's response was to produce a design that incorporated all of the client's requirements in a workable building with a few creative additions. The look of the building would be very much in a style that has become typically The TreeHouse Company. (The round treehouse with a conical roof is a type that the company has built many times and the design had evolved into something of a TreeHouse Company classic.) Guests would climb a spiral staircase hidden behind the treehouse and step onto a small balcony, which would be sheltered by its own charming peaked roof. A door would lead into the treehouse's main room, which was to be laid out around a central dining table held in three boughs of the ash. Light would flood in through thirteen windows equally spaced around the walls. To one side would be the small kitchen and to the other fitted benches beneath five of the windows. At the front, double doors were to lead out onto the large veranda. The building, including the veranda, would measure nearly twenty-five feet in diameter, spacious enough to accommodate eight guests for dinner, plus serving staff.

Because of the garden's historic status planning permission had to be procured before the build could begin, with local authorities requiring to approve detailed plans. As the building had been designed with a great deal of empathy to its surroundings and was intended to enhance the landscape, permission was granted without further complications and four The TreeHouse Company craftsmen arrived on site.

The treehouse took several months to complete, much longer than most of the buildings that the company undertakes. In part this was due to the amount of care taken during the build. Although the craftsmen are always prudent with the tree and its environment, in this case the build was even more sensitive. Scaffolding was erected to minimize the amount of climbing in the tree and painstaking efforts were made not to traumatize it in any way. The length of time needed was, however, mostly due to the complexity of the structure. Fitting thirteen windows in a treehouse is no easy task and the installation of the required amenities was also labor intensive. For example, the lavatory had to be connected to the mains waste pipes and this entailed a lot more work than is usual for a less well-appointed treehouse. Disguising the plumbing was also necessary, and was achieved by encasing the pipes that run down the trunk of the tree in timber carved to look like the tree's bark.

The finished building is a very aesthetically pleasing treehouse with half-shingled walls in cedar and a cedar-shingled roof. The decking and window frames are, again, cedar. Left natural, this wood will weather beautifully over the next three or four years, eventually turning a handsome silvery gray, similar in color to the ash tree's bark. Like the tree itself, the wood will change shade during different seasons, turning a dark brown in winter and when wet. This means that the treehouse will eventually blend even more within its setting than it does now.

The interior walls are finished with highly polished tongue-and-groove lining in red pine, while the floor is of polished cedar. In the center, the table—a piece of naturally formed, polished ash—is fitted on sliding brackets that allow movement in the boughs while the table remains still. Heating and subtle lighting make this a comfortable room all year round. As you would expect for a treehouse of this quality it has been finished inside to the highest standards, with furniture and décor tastefully selected and no expense spared.

The client is ecstatic with the new addition to the grounds, and entertains guests and business associates here on a regular basis. The kitchen, while perfectly adequate for preparing relatively simple meals is not intended for the kind of gourmet dinners that are an everyday event up in the treehouse and is mostly used to warm dishes that have been prepared in the extensive kitchens of the main house. While the treehouse is an amazing and luxurious space in its own right it is the setting that really makes it such a wonderful place to be. No dining room in the main house could ever offer guests comparable views out across these immaculate gardens, or give such a sense of being so close to nature. Eating from a table held in the branches of a tree, surrounded by foliage is an experience that no guest here is likely to forget, and one that is difficult to communicate in words. The smell of the cedar, the proximity of the tree's canopy, and the sense of serenity mean that no dinner here can be truly formal; you are a guest of the tree, and formality is impossible with such a host.

Designer: **Gordon Brown**

Craftsmen: **Willie McCubbin (team leader),
Dax Druce, Peter Tudhope, Jim Wales**

Dimensions: **25' diameter (plus veranda and balcony)**

Materials: **10" x 3" Scandinavian pine (joists and
structural)**

Cedar decking

Cedar floorboards (interior)

Cedar shingles (roof and exterior walls)

**Vertical tongue-and-groove boarding in red pine
(interior lining)**

Neoprene (collars around the trunk)

2" x 2" cedar (balustrade)

Solid cedar door

3" x 2" cedar timber (window frames)

Double glazed windows (toughened)

12" x 3" cedar timber (spiral staircase)

Large shaped piece of ash (dining table)

THE CONFERENCE TREEHOUSE

With world quality services, state of the art communications, and no distractions, this vast treehouse is the perfect venue for a high-level business conference.

Opposite page: **One of the world's most exclusive retreats for corporate meetings and entertainment.**

At the northern tip of Scotland, a good many miles from any large town, is a fifteenth century tower that houses one of the world's most exclusive hotels. Guests come here for privacy and the romance of the spectacular landscape, as well as the amazing views of the Northern Lights. Ackergill Tower Hotel also has a reputation as a venue for very confidential conferences. The chiefs of some of the world's most successful companies come here to discuss strategy in absolute seclusion in what must be one of the world's most expensive, and expansive, treehouses.

The brainchild of the hotel's owners, the treehouse is an outstanding, unique achievement. It boasts a commercial kitchen and seating for forty, bathrooms, and full

Right: **Flying into Wick International airport, the view of Ackergill Tower must be one of Scotland's finest—the fifteenth century medieval castle overlooks the Pentland Firth at the very northern tip of Britain.**

Garden House

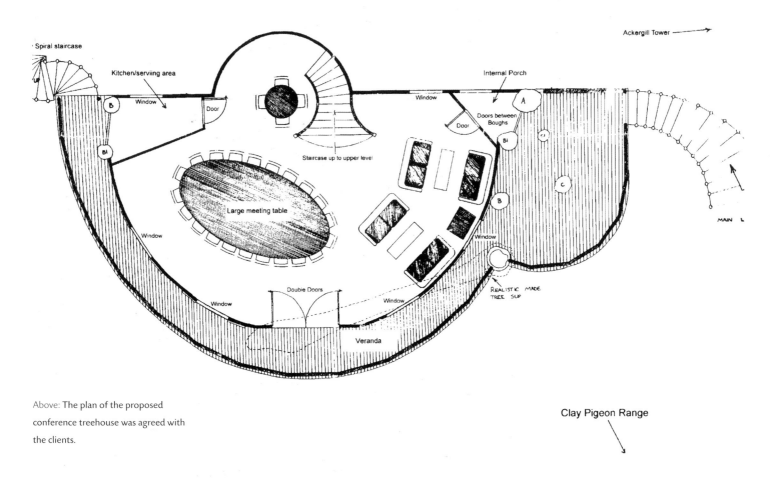

Above: **The plan of the proposed conference treehouse was agreed with the clients.**

Clay Pigeon Range

conference facilities for thirty-two delegates (including internet access for each, video conferencing, interactive white boards, DVD, and satellite—all hidden until needed). It even has its own observatory, complete with telescope, in the roof. Unsurprisingly it is booked up years in advance.

The client approached the author with the initial idea for the treehouse in the summer of 2001. They knew the specifications of the building they wanted, but the design was to take a year of ideas and discussions before being settled upon. The final concept drawings and computer generated simulations showed a relatively low, circular building with a conical roof interrupted at its peak by a small tower (the observatory), with its own conical roof. Incorporating six trees into its structure it would have a curved dormer covered in rounded

copper shingles over double entrance doors, the latter a reference to the hotel's mermaid logo.

The trees that would host the massive structure are highly unusual. Wild sycamores of about 150 years in age, they had grown in an old walled garden where once the castle's vegetables were cultivated. Sheltered from the prevailing winds off the nearby sea, they had grown normally in the rich soil until their branches had reached the top of the wall, at which point they had been blown and shaped by the winds, producing very strange, though not unattractive, trees. However, their flexible branches would not be easy to incorporate into the building. Although the trees were established and sturdy even six could not be expected to support such an enormous building alone, and stilts also had to be incorporated into the design.

Right: It is unusual to find large trees in such windy climes as the north of Scotland. These sycamores grew up protected by the walled garden, and once they reached a considerable height, the strong sea breezes gave fantastical shapes to the topmost branches.

Right: The CAD drawing produced months before the treehouse construction was started bears a striking resemblance to the finished building.

Left: Although set in the rustic surroundings of a sycamore grove, meetings conducted inside the treehouse are high-tech, with video conferencing, satellite communication, and instant Internet access, all installed to make treetop business life run smoothly.

Below left: The copper tiles over the arched roof above the main doors remind you of the mermaid's fish scales that are the emblem of Ackergill Tower. The theme is reflected in the weather vane that sits at the top of the tower of the treehouse.

Construction began in November 2002, a time when the trees were dormant and would be less traumatized by the extensive building work going on around them. Due to the location, every single piece of equipment and material needed to be brought in by truck, which caused a great deal of frustration, and such was the care taken over construction that heavy equipment was not allowed on site in case it compacted the trees' root systems. With the top of the tower reaching forty-two feet above the ground, and high winds whipping around the framework, scaffolding needed to be erected. However, with six people working on it full time, the treehouse gradually took shape over the cold Scottish winter months.

The finished wooden building is a semi-circular structure of cedar, willow, and red pine, with windows and a balcony stretching all the way round. Doors and window frames are in hardwood, the roof is topped with cedar shingles, and it is finished with Volcanic Ash wood stain to help it blend with the surrounding trees. As you approach it you can hear music playing in the trees. Mount the spiral staircase and stand on the deck and you will witness spectacular views of Ackergill village on one side and the sea and castle on the other. Entry to the treehouse is through arched double doors, and the "V" of two trees. Inside the scale of the treehouse is staggering. The conference room is calm and airy in soft creams and beiges, with a high vaulted ceiling and

Right: The largest treehouse in Europe
and a special place to visit.

light flooding in from the windows on all sides, complemented by discreet lighting in the ceiling above. Interior timbers have been washed lightly with green that doesn't disguise the grain of the wood. Afghan rugs cover the polished wooden floor, and a table is covered in fine linen, with green water-glasses, fresh fruit, cheese, and shortbread laid out for delegates. A huge tree trunk runs through the conference suite and out of the cedar shingled roof.

Your eye is drawn naturally upward to an astrodome roof, where a telescope tracks the position of the stars. This is unlike any conference room anywhere else—utterly peaceful, and yet tremendously exciting. Off the main conference hall is the kitchen; fitted out in stainless steel it is fully capable of producing cuisine of the finest quality for up to forty, with enough room for both chefs and waiting staff. There is also a changing room for removing wet clothes and muddy boots and male and female bathrooms, luxuriously appointed and fully ventilated.

The treehouse itself is completely at ease in its environment, designed to reflect the architecture of the main buildings as well as harmonize with its surroundings. In a space like this business is not mixed with pleasure, but becomes a pleasure. There is a tranquility to the atmosphere that is entirely conducive to creativity and effective communication.

Designer: **Gordon Brown / John Harris**

Craftsmen: **Willie McCubbin (team leader),**
Dax Druce, Brian Keown, Stuart Carmichael,
George Grossart, Peter Tudhope

Dimensions: **75' x 36' (with veranda)**
50' x 30' (treehouse)

Materials: **10" x 3" timber (joists and structural)**
6" x 1" hardwood decking
6" x 1" tongue-and-groove floorboards (interior)
4" x ¾" timber (interior lining)
6" x ¾" log-effect timber (exterior walls)
Cedar shingles
Neoprene (collar around the trunk)
Willow (balustrade)
3" x 2" hardwood timber (window frames)
Double glazed windows
Wood stain

TREEHOUSES AT CHELSEA

Each year The TreeHouse Company creates a complete treehouse just for the Chelsea Flower Show.

Opposite page: **Chelsea Flower Show 2003, with a proud stag guarding the fantasy treehouse.**

Every year in May the British Royal Horticultural Society presents the Chelsea Flower Show in Chelsea, London. Just to exhibit here is one of the most prized and prestigious accolades in the world of gardening, and is by invitation of the RHS only. Over five days in excess of 150,000 people, including nearly 1,000 members of the press, will visit, making it the most important garden showcase in the world. The 600 exhibitors represent the most distinguished landscapers and gardeners in the world. Cutting-edge architectural gardeners rub shoulders with bonsai masters, with everyone competing fiercely for the prized medals. The atmosphere in the days leading up to the show is sheer bedlam, with every one of the exhibitors racing against time to have their showpiece finished. Nevertheless there is a great sense of camaraderie, and the exhibitors come to know each other very well over the years.

The TreeHouse Company have been honored to be invited back every year since 2000. Each time the company designs a new and original treehouse to construct in the boughs of the same tree they use every year, a venerable old horse chestnut near Chelsea Bridge and overlooking the River Thames. It

Left: In 2001 the red horse-chestnut tree played host to an art glass window treehouse. An elegant and petite building with a shingled exterior, it was designed and built especially for the show. Many people who enjoyed a relaxing seat on the swing underneath were inspired to become treehouse owners.

Left: The beautiful red horse-chestnut tree, the home of The TreeHouse Company's showpiece each year at the Chelsea Flower Show.

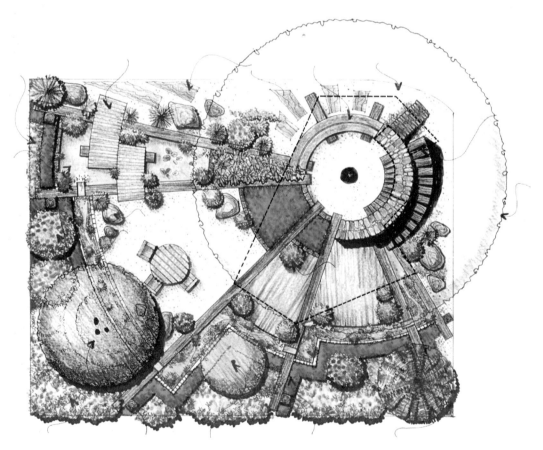

Left: The treehouse garden at the 2002 Chelsea Flower Show brought together The TreeHouse Company craftsmen and landscape architects to create a Malaysian style showpiece that was awarded a prestigious Silver Gilt medal for its innovative design.

is the most important show of the year for the company and one that invariably leads to a flood of new orders, so the treehouse needs to be of the company's best, even though it will only last a few days.

The treehouse is planned rigorously in advance as there is only ten days allotted to actually build it before the show opens. There are also strict regulations regarding the tree itself, which must not be damaged in any way. Not a single screw or bolt must damage its bark; when the treehouse is removed the tree must be in the same pristine condition as it was before. This means that the structure must be either suspended from the upper branches with slings and wire, supported by stilts from below, or a combination of both. With thousands of people wanting to climb into the treehouse over the week of the show, great pains must also be taken to make sure that the building is safe and stable. Indeed, it is inspected by the local authorities before the show begins to ensure that it meets local safety standards. However, there is one benefit to be had. As the treehouse need only last a week it does not have to be completely weatherproof, and does not need the same close attention to finishing details as a normal build. Once the show is over the company has two days to remove the treehouse completely.

2000

The TreeHouse Company was first invited to the Chelsea Flower Show in the wake of the newspaper feature on the treehouse on page 78. For the first show the company did not want to be over-ambitious, and were unfamiliar with the tree, so a simple deck was planned, reaching out on both sides of the tree on two levels. This was not a treehouse proper, but it served to fire the imaginations of visitors, showing that trees could be used in ways that most people would never consider. Those who climbed up top the leafy deck were first surprised to find that the view from the deck was quite amazing. Their next response

was that after walking around the crowded show in warm sunshine the deck was a calm and relaxing place, shaded by the tree's canopy and cooled by a gentle breeze.

Despite the simplicity of the exhibit it was a very successful show for The TreeHouse Company, and they also realized the potential of the tree. Strong and sturdy there was a wealth of space up in the branches, easily enough to hold a full-sized treehouse. It was decided that the next year the company would show what it was capable of.

2001

The second year at Chelsea brought gasps of wonder from the 7,200 visitors who climbed into the branches of the horse chestnut to look

Right: The interior is true to the style of a Bali Longhouse, where the walls are left open to provide ventilation. The materials used were a cultural fusion of weathered timber, bamboo, sequoia, driftwood, and willow.

Left: The interior of the 2002 treehouse was rich with colors and textures, the Gothic style windows softened with elaborate fabrics.

Below: Constructed almost entirely from lightweight bamboo and raised on stilts, the thatched roof of the treehouse was almost completely camouflaged underneath the drapery of the towering horse-chestnut tree.

around The TreeHouse Company's magical little treehouse. The structure was given a backdrop of wild flowers and sculpted wildlife by Gold Medal winning gardener Jacquie Gordon.

The treehouse was an attractive combination of half height, fancy shaped shingles in Canadian cedar with art glass windows, and a veranda. A swing was installed below and there was a basket on a pulley for pulling up many bottles of wine. Access to the veranda was by spiral staircase and a straight staircase was built to the rear so that visitors could walk through and down without causing a crush.

2002

A completely different approach was taken the following year, with an elegant treehouse created to look like a traditional Bali long house, set in its own serene garden. The treehouse received high acclaim from professionals and public alike and was one of the most talked about exhibits, being awarded a silver-gilt medal.

The building combined a variety of beautiful woods, including weathered timber, bamboo, sequoia, driftwood, and willow. A curved staircase gave access onto large open decks with water running down rills on the edge of each stair tread. Strong bamboo balustrades

Above: A feature dormer window on the 2003 treehouse. The building, erected in just ten days takes the concept of a fantasy treehouse to the limit.

Above: The large feature window made an excellent place for a padded window seat on the inside.

Above: The front balcony featured
attractive curved balustrade rails.

Above: A swing was installed below the
TreeHouse, the perfect place for a
princess to rest.

ran around the deck areas, with bamboo roll blinds creating a
screening that was enhanced by a traditional oak shingle roof.

The garden was designed to reflect a tranquil journey ascend-
ing up into the treehouse, its ambience created by using natural
products such as reclaimed timber and drystone. Water cascaded
down the treehouse through a series of chutes and rills into a
waterfall pond.

2003

The year of writing saw the most ambitious Chelsea project to date, a
complete fairy tale castle with copper shingled spires that really caused

a stir. Inspired by Bavarian castles the building comprised of three
rooms, three balconies, dormer windows, a bowed balustrade, carved
detailing on supporting stilts, and Gothic style windows and doors.
The turrets could be climbed by spiral staircase and in the main turret
room was hung a beautiful chandelier. At the top of the treehouse was
a special balcony for invited guests and VIPs. The exterior was stained
a mahogany color that perfectly matched the pink of the tree's blossom, while window frames were painted green to match the foliage.
Below was a swing, which was reserved for the use of The TreeHouse
Company's very own princess.

A TREEHOUSE GALLERY

Imagine sitting high up in the branches in your own treehouse.

Opposite page: With a Mediterranean feel this children's treehouse is stained in pastel greens and yellows.

Below: Its often at night that a treehouse looks its most magical. Simple lighting can have an extraordinary effect.

With over 500 now finished, this book cannot hope to show all of the amazing treehouses that The TreeHouse Company have built in a few short years. However, the following pages are devoted to a careful selection of a few more. Chosen to represent a wide range of designs, and show the kind of structures that are possible, we hope it inspires you to take a look at your own garden and wonder just what might be possible.

Above: The treehouse appears to fly high above you as you pass below along the footpath.

Left: A rustic retreat, this treehouse is constructed mainly from cedar with "waney" edged boards. Blending in with its surroundings, it hides the children as they play behind the tree canopy.

Above: Set high on a mountainside this boat-inspired treehouse seems to float in the air and moves gently as the wind blows.

Right: Over twenty feet high this covered platform is a long climb up. However, it is well worth the effort as the views over distant Paris are revealed from the deck.

Left: Inspired by Hans Christian Anderson, this cedar shingled crooked spire roof looks just like a witch's hat. The totally round walls, twisty staircase, and natural twig balustrade all add to the fairy-tale effect.

Above: On a nice sunny day there is
nothing better than hanging around in
the treehouse.

Left: Set in the grounds of an old Oast
House, this treehouse was designed
with a desk built into the semi-circular
tower. Fully equipped with heating and
electricity, it is used as a part-time
home office.

Left: Linked to a deck for the adults by
a rope bridge, this children's treehouse
is thatched with a South African water
reed, and has feature carving around
the front door. There is also a rear
door leading out onto a balcony
looking over the fields beyond.

Above: In the evening light the tree
and treehouse catch the last of the
sun's golden rays.

Right: With a distinctly Polynesian feel
this treehouse has bamboo blinds and
large open spaces; plenty of lamps give
it a comfortable look after dark.

Left: The two balconies which catch the morning and evening sun make this the idea spot to catch a nap or read the newspapers.

Right: Inspired by the Enid Blyton book where a collection of creatures make their ram-shackle dwelling winding up and around the old gnarled trunk.

Below: A family in Berkshire compromised in the design of their family treehouse, and split the building into two towers. The taller one is for the children to host parties in, and the lower for the adults to enjoy picnics.

Below right: A treehouse with a dovecot, overlooking Lake Como in Italy.

BUILDING YOUR OWN TREEHOUSE

Opposite page: High in a giant Oak Tree this adults treehouse is not easy to see except for the tall spiral staircase in front of the tree trunk.

Below: Inspired by the Ewoks from Star Wars an Ewok village has been created around the lake shore.

Above: "I feel as if this tree knows everything I ever think of when I sit here. When I come back to it, I never have to remind it of anything; I begin just where I left off."

Willa Cather, *Pioneers!*

A Treehouse for all Seasons

Built in a perfect rural setting to look good in every season, a treehouse that is a model for anyone planning to build their own.

Opposite page: There's nothing like the sense of achievement of actually building a treehouse, especially when it looks as magical and fairy tale as this one.

The author was first approached for this picturesque little treehouse soon after the company started business. Having had a treehouse as a child the client wanted a simple retreat for herself, where she could relax with a book away from telephones and visitors. However, after excited initial discussions nothing was heard from the client and it was assumed that she had decided against the project. After a year though a letter arrived from her daughter. Her mother had died and the family was looking for a suitable memorial to her. Knowing how much she had loved the idea of her treehouse reading room they wanted to go ahead with the building, instead making it into a playroom for her beloved grandchildren. Although the result is certainly not the grandest treehouse that his company have been

Right: A dusting of snow transforms the setting into a winter wonderland. The treehouse hides under heavy boughs laden with powdery frost.

Above: Perfectly integrated with its beech host the treehouse is well supported with large knee bracers, and a sturdy balustrade ensures safety.

Left: Surrounded by leaves of amber, lime, and rust, a small door is hidden away on the treehouse balcony in the middle of the beech tree.

This page: The idea of a secret treehouse appealed to this family. They asked for a small building that you might imagine an animal living inside and this hand drawing was agreed as the design.

Left: The treehouse was painted silvery-gray and dark green so that it would reflect the tone of the beech bark and blend into the changing colors of the tree canopy at all times of the year.

involved with, this has become one of the author's favorites, perfectly suited to its environment and looking stunning all year round. It is also a good model for anyone planning their own, and for that reason there is a more detailed explanation of the design and construction here, in order to give a sense of how the treehouse took shape.

The possibilities of a beautiful 140-year-old beech tree, about 200 yards from the main house were apparent as soon as it was seen from the driveway to the country home of the clients. Fortunately they were of the same opinion, adding that they wanted the treehouse to be subtle and sympathetic to the rest of the grounds. They did not want the tree to be overwhelmed by the structure, and also requested that the treehouse would also look attractive during all four seasons. During the first conversation the author was asked for "Nothing too grand or sophisticated, but something close to the spirit of what a treehouse is all about. Something simple for the children, that will fit in with the surroundings and not dominate too much." The author pointed out to them the strong, unusually symmetrical, "V" shape of the two boughs where the trunk split about eight feet from the ground, between which could be fitted the main door. As the family wanted the treehouse hidden from view of the main house this would work wonderfully. A small veranda could be built at the front, with the treehouse itself tucked behind the fork of the tree.

During an initial survey the girth of the trunk was measured and the trunk, branches, and roots inspected for any signs of weakness or rot. With a surveyor's staff, the height of each branch was also measured, and a map sketched of the direction in which they were growing. The author climbed a ladder up into the "V" of the beech tree, and stood there, trying to visualize what sort of platform space the tree might hold. Because the tree is a beech, it would look quite different at the changing of each season. At the time, in summer, it was a rich bushy green, but soon it would turn yellow and then golden brown in fall, and finally stand almost bare in the wintertime. The treehouse colors should be chosen to look good at all times of the year, and the author thought a silvery gray or pale-green stained wooden treehouse might best suit the tree. The veranda should be slightly higher than the house, giving the impression that you would be walking down into the room. The survey showed the tree to be a fine specimen in perfect health and had grown as if to suggest the treehouse that it would like, so having been refined and properly

planned the author's initial impression was accepted immediately.

Construction began at the beginning of a perfect autumnal October, with a tarpaulin spread below the tree to protect the grass and a tape perimeter around the site to deter children from approaching during construction. The simple single rung ladder up to the treehouse was the first thing to be built so that it could be used to bring tools and materials to the platform. The ladder was fixed into the ground with concrete and bolted to the tree-trunk. The main frame of the platform was then laid out using pressure treated Scandinavian pine. There were two platforms to construct, both quite awkward shapes, so the angles of the wood were cut down on the ground. The 6 "x 2" joists were then hoisted up using a rope pulley attached to the tree. Once the platform was in place, ropes held it steady while a spirit level was used to ensure that the floor was even. Galvanized eight inch bolts were then used to attach the platform to the tree. Only when the knee bracers had been fixed to the platform were the ropes removed. The treehouse began to take form with the decking of the platform floor. The front veranda was completed first, with ridged decking designed to be non-slip in wet weather. A safe balustrade was then built around the platform using one and a half inch dowels cut to the same length. Drilled into the bottom and top rail, this made a solid pine balustrade. On the opposite side of the tree, smooth tongue-and-groove floorboards were fitted together to form the treehouse floor. The craftsmen were careful to scribe the floorboards around the tree, leaving room for it to grow (later the gap between tree and floorboards was covered up with coconut rope).

The next day saw the frame for the treehouse walls being built and placed. The treehouse is quite simple, formed from two shaped walls and one low back wall, so there were only three frames to build from 4" x 2" timber, with gaps left for the windows. The walls were constructed down on the ground and then hoisted up to the platform where they were firmly glued to add extra strength and screwed into position. Once the frame had been assembled, it needed to be covered in vertical exterior boards, again leaving gaps around the trunk for the tree to keep on growing. Because of the sloping roof down to the back wall, every board had to be individually measured and cut to size.

The next job was the roof, which as a relatively simple design, was not too difficult to complete. Craftsmen in safety harnesses

Above: Instead of a chimney, the treehouse has huge branches coming out of the cedar shingle roof. You can see here how the tree is allowed to keep on moving and growing by using a neoprene collar to wrap around the branch.

marine plyboard were next screwed onto the roof for waterproofing. (Marine ply is used on boats, so works well for waterproofing outdoor buildings.) A neoprene collar, made from a rubbery material similar to a wetsuit, was fitted onto the tree trunk and left to "float" on the marine ply so the trunk could still move. The neoprene prevents rain from getting inside the treehouse, while expanding as the tree itself grows. At this stage it was decided that the roof should extend in between the tree branches to provide a shelter over the door so that water would not run onto the heads of children entering the treehouse. It is quite normal to re-think even computer-aided design images during the build. Blueprints are always an excellent guide, but when you start work on a site you have to adapt to the needs of the tree.

The next two tasks were the shingling of the roof and staining of the woodwork, after which the treehouse looked close to finished. Canadian cedar shingles gave the roof a rustic look, particularly as the shingles used were all different sizes, giving an irregular pattern. Cedar is an excellent wood for roofing, as it has its own oil and doesn't need to be treated. It will also change color in different weather conditions, just as trees do, and will be incredibly enduring, lasting for at least twenty-five years. The shingling was started at the bottom, and worked upward in layered rows, nailing all the way up and round the tree trunk that protruding through the treehouse roof. The last few shingles were fitted snugly over the neoprene collar, holding it in place. While one craftsman worked on the roof another undertook the messy job of staining the veranda, deck, and balcony, giving the treehouse its finished color and protecting it from the elements.

Having left space in the walls for them to be fitted, the windows were the next to be put in. It is possible to buy old window frames from salvage yards, but in this case they were crafted from scratch to the dimensions of the spaces left in the original frame. Each window frame was made on the ground, stained dark green, and then fitted with unbreakable polycarbonate. (You should never use glass in a treehouse because of the risk of a branch hitting against it.) The special door to the treehouse, fitting between the two main branches was the last construction job. Several tongue-and-groove boards were fitted together to make a square, then batons were screwed onto the back to make a solid shape. A template of the space the door was to fill between the branches was cut from plywood, gradually scribed

bolted roofing beams across the treehouse frame and strips of wood six inches apart and running in the same direction as the joists were used to fill in the gaps between the larger beams. (It is interesting to note that this method of construction is very similar to that used for a normal house roof, except for one thing: there is a tree trunk coming through the roof.) Small batons of wood were then "dwanged" around the trunk (that is the large joints are filled with smaller pieces, in this case forming a shape around the tree trunk) leaving a gap for sway and movement of the tree. Sheets of thick

Inside, the family later added all manner of wall hangings and pictures and toys are also hung from the walls to keep the room tidy. This is a space for fun and play though and there is no sense of formality. Despite the fact that there is no electricity or heating the treehouse is in constant use, and not only by the children.

The end result is a simple treehouse perfectly adapted to its use and to its environment. Relatively easy to build, it is proportionally correct and uses the tree's own shape in its design and construction, which means that the finished treehouse does not detract from the beauty of its host. The huge beech is a focal point in the countryside, but the treehouse has been designed and built so carefully that, while being visible, it seems an organic part of the landscape.

Above: The "V" between the two boughs of the beech makes for an unusual door frame.

away at to get the exact shape. The template was then traced around onto the door and a jigsaw used to cut out the shape. After fitting two big "T" hinges onto the tree, it was lifted into position.

The final day of building was spent in finishing touches—furniture consisting of two little stools painted blue, and a small seat for the branch on the veranda; a rope-ladder for the children, which was attached top and bottom with timber pegs; and carved fascia boards to hide the roof beams of the building. The latter were scalloped along the bottom using a paint tin to trace out a curvy shape. Finally, little steps to help the children up and over the tree branch to enter their treehouse were made. One more detail was added; a sun shape on the door. The site was then cleared, with attention being paid to finding any small screws or nails that might have gone astray.

Designer: John Harris

Craftsmen: John Harris (team leader),
    Willie McCubbin

Dimensions: 10' x 16' (with veranda)
    10' feet x 8' (treehouse)

Materials: 6" x 2" Scandinavian pine, rough sawn
    (joists and structural)

Knee bracers

Non-slip ridged decking

Tongue-and-groove floorboards (interior)

3" vertical tongue-and-groove boarding
    (exterior walls and door)

Cedar shingles

Neoprene (collar around the trunk)

1½" round dowling (balustrade)

2" x 2" timber (window frames)

Polycarbonate windows

2" x 3" timber (ladder)

Wood stain

BUILDING YOUR OWN TREEHOUSE

Your own tree-building. For them, for you, for everybody. The only limit is your imagination.

You may decide after looking at the treehouses in this book that you would like to build your own. This is a wonderful idea! There is nothing better than a treehouse except a treehouse that you have made with your own hands. However, before you race out to buy the tools, do take into consideration that you will need a good level of DIY knowledge to begin with. treehouse construction is challenging and can be dangerous if all the proper precautions are not taken. If you do not think that you are equipped for the task, then find somebody who is, and work together. Talk to the staff at your local building suppliers or hardware outlet and familiarize yourself with the wood, tools, and materials you will need to use. Unless you are a tree expert, you will almost certainly need to speak to a qualified arborist about the health of your proposed tree-site. As you will see, the key to good

Right: A treehouse such as this is a big project for an amateur, taking many weekends. However, the result will be well worth the effort.

treehouse construction is in the planning. This small guide is a good jumping off point for amateur builders, with ten steps to show you how to get started. Remember to read everything thoroughly before you begin to build.

Before you start though, remember that the author has three objectives when it comes to designing and constructing any treehouse, it is strongly suggest that you apply these as well, in the same order of priority.

1. Safety before anything else, climbing a tree requires a lot of care, building in a tree needs a lot more. Always be careful, and if in doubt find a different, safer, way of approaching the task at hand.

2. Look after your host, don't do any thing to damage or stress the tree in which you are building.

3. Aesthetics are very important, a visually unappealing treehouse can be an eyesore. Make sure your design is sympathetic to the tree and the environment.

Above: Tarzan meets Swiss family Robinson. The Baker family wanted a really adventurous treehouse for their children, and they got it—thirty feet above ground level on the slope of a cluster of lime trees.

Right: Treehouses are the ultimate adventure playground for children, a magical place where they have their own den to play in with no rules to spoil their fun. Running, screaming, and using the imagination all seem compulsory activities.

STEP ONE

CHOOSING THE BEST TREE FOR YOUR TREEHOUSE

It is important that that you spend some time designing the structure of your dream treehouse. But before you bring out the graph paper and pencils remember that your finished treehouse is going to greatly depend on the tree that you choose to build in. You should always let the values of the tree determine the possibilities for building. Whether you have one tree or many to choose from it is the tree that will determine the final result more than any other factor.

Begin by spending time surveying the tree or trees in your garden or on your land—in particular inspect the roots, the trunk, and the branches for any disease or weakness such as cracks, a leaning trunk, loose bark, sinking branches, shallow roots, rot, or fungus. Also examine the branch connections—V-shaped branches are not as strong as U-shaped branches. Load bearing branches should be at least six inches in diameter. Remember that rot and disease can be hidden, and

Above: Finding the perfect tree is what all treehouse builders yearn for, for the first timer a simple hardwood, like this semi-mature beech is ideal.

Above: This stunning oak tree was a good choice for would-be treehouse craftsmen—every one of its seventeen branches were incorporated into the design, without a single bough or twig being removed during the construction. It is always strongly recommended to consult a certified arborist when choosing the tree in which you intend to build. Many trees have hidden dangers such as damaged roots or hidden rot, and this might eliminate their chance of being used to host a treehouse.

Above: Don't set your sights too high on your first treehouse, it gets harder as you go higher!

Right: With the door between the boughs, it feels as if you are walking into the tree itself.

even the seemingly healthiest species can hold hidden hazards. If you are unfamiliar with the needs of trees, it will be of great benefit to consult a certified arborist, who will be able to determine the health of your trees, this is also a good opportunity to remove any dead branches. Always remember that your tree is a living host, and will need your care and maintenance both during and after the treehouse construction. It is likely that you will have to provide additional watering to the ground as the treehouse structure may block out natural rainwater for the tree.

The best shaped trees for treehouse construction are those that resemble an upturned palm, as these have a natural space in the crown of the tree for holding the body of the treehouse. The best varieties of European tree that The TreeHouse Company most commonly build in are beech, oak, ash, chestnut, sycamore, lime, and larger pines and spruces, however most species of tree will be capable of holding a treehouse. Whatever type of tree you choose, remember that it must be semi-mature or mature and in good health. The location of the tree is obviously of great importance too.

Don't worry too much about trying to achieve a great height in your treehouse design, especially if you are making the building for

the use of children or if it's your first attempt at treehouse construction. Some of the most spectacular treehouses are smaller, lower structures, and, generally, trees are more hospitable to this type of structure. In order to build high up in a tree you will need an extremely large, strong tree with powerful upper branches. Building nearer to the ground reduces the risk of the treehouse acting as a sail in high winds and possibly damaging both itself and anything that it supports.

The first question to ask yourself is "What will my treehouse be used for?" If it is going to be a children's treehouse, your dimensions will be a lot smaller than, say, an adult office space. It's often useful the consult the rest of the family to establish what they may want to use the treehouse for. It is also important to think about the longer term use of a treehouse. Remember that properly constructed and maintained a treehouse will last for many years, even decades, and therefore it may well have a changing role as time passes. Think also about the direction the treehouse will be approached from and the direction of the sun and where it hits the tree at different times of day.

Take these things into account at an early stage when you are designing your treehouse.

Don't forget to consult your neighbors about your proposed plans—if they can see your treehouse from their property, then it becomes their business too. Treehouses should never be situated where they can cause a nuisance, for example overlooking someone else's garden or into a neighbor's house, so avoid windows facing other properties).

Treehouses are not meant to be permanent structures, and therefore in most cases planning permission should not be needed, but it is always better to check with your local authority. However, if your treehouse is discrete, well designed, and not interfering with neighbors or passing motorists planning permission will usually be granted when it is required.

If your tree is subject to a tree preservation order (TPO) you should always ask your local Tree Officer first and gain his approval to construct.

The TreeHouse Company regularly constructs in trees with TPO's and works closely with local authorities. Tree Officers are now aware that the techniques used do not damage the tree in any way and no branches are removed from the tree at any time.

STEP TWO
THE MASTER PLANNING LIST

Try to have all the materials you need for building the treehouse assembled before you begin along with a precise plan of how everything will fit together—that way you will know the dimensions of all the objects such as windows, doors, rope-bridges, and ladders, that you are going to fix to your treehouse frame. These are the main points that you will need to consider before you commence building:

SAFETY HARNESS

It is paramount that you make sure you will be safe throughout the treehouse installation. You will be working on roofs and platforms high above the ground and finding a sure footing may be difficult. Accidents do happen, so before you begin, always fit a safety line for yourself and any other builders. If you have never used a safety harness before, now is the time to learn how! Your local climbing instructor will be able to give you a quick lesson, as will an arborist. Attach a tree-climber's saddle to your body. This can have one static line tied to a strong main branch high in the tree so that if you slip, the rope will catch you. You can also attach your main line to another fixed line with a climbers knot, so that by pulling the loose end of the rope you can move up to the correct height. Slide the knot up to anchor yourself, and squeeze the knot to loosen it and descend. Have a practice at your knots before you start work up the tree.

PULLEYS

The tree should be able to provide the leverage to help you hoist all your equipment into the air so long as the upper branches are sufficiently strong. Use a branch directly above where you want to lift items, about ten feet above where your roof level will be. Make sure that there are no hanging branches that will interfere with your lines. You can use a block and tackle or attach a rope and metal pulley. You may be able to climb up the tree to tie this on, or if working at a lower level a ladder may be sufficient. If not, you can attach a bag filled with pebbles to one end of the rope and use this to hook one of the tree limbs. You will find that a bowline knot is useful for attaching a line to a branch. If in doubt about where to purchase specialist equipment, contact your local arborist or climbing shop.

Left: Your safety, and the safety of others, has to be paramount during the construction of the treehouse. Safety harnesses are used for safe tree-climbing, and courses are available to learn how to use them from professional climbing centers. As on any building site, wear a hard hat, and use protective ear-muffs during loud drilling work. Working on a roof can be a potentially dangerous business. A tree climber's saddle is a type of safety harness that allows you to move around the top of the treehouse with the secure knowledge that you will be caught by the rope if you accidentally slip.

THE PLATFORM

Before you start cutting the frame for your treehouse walls exactly the same size as your platform, you'll want to consider how you are going to assign your platform space. Balconies and veranda areas also give an outdoor space, and should be considered alongside the initial platform space. Would you like a balcony on one side, or a veranda running the whole way round the house? You will have to measure your frame to leave room for these features. On graph paper, use a suitable scale to design the layout of your platform frame. Remember to account for the width of the walls, and a space for the balustrades to run the perimeter of the veranda. At this stage you also want to think about the exits and entrances you will be using, for example where a staircase or ladder will join the platform frame. Deciding how to have entry into your treehouse is a major factor. Do you need a wide staircase for carrying up trays of drinks? Or will a ladder for the use of adventurous children suffice?

THE ROOF

Take head-space into account at the planning stage. Draw a plan of the dimensions of your treehouse frame as a working model. If you lay out a lifesize version of your treehouse frame on the ground with string it will give you a realistic idea of your dimensions. This will also help you to visualize how steep the pitch of your roof is going to be. You will also want to decide whether you would like a covered balcony on the treehouse deck, and if so, incorporate this into the roof design.

WINDOWS

Don't forget to incorporate space in the frame for your windows and doors. You may already have a door you wish to use, or perhaps intend to make your own windows. Remember that the size of your windows and the door will dictate the spacing of your wall frames. It is also a good idea to stand on the platform and estimate an eye-level view for either an adult or a child so that you can measure the correct level for the windows to be fixed and of course take advantage of the new views. Never use glass in a treehouse, as it may break as the treehouse moves and twists or if a branch bangs against it.

ROPE-BRIDGES

There may only be one access point around the tree platform that is

Above: **Carrying heavy pieces of timber up a ladder is not the most sensible idea. Instead, stay safe on the ground and use a hoist to lift beams into the tree into the waiting hands of a fellow workmate.**

suitable for installing a rope bridge. You will need to have a tree nearby that is strong enough to support a landing platform. Your platform frame must face the landing platform straight on, and not at an angle.

INTERIORS

You may wish to think at this early stage about possible interior furnishings such as raised bed bunks or creating a space for a dining table to sit around the trunk. This will give you a better idea of how much floor space is needed when laying out the design on graph paper.

ELECTRICITY

Consider whether you wish the treehouse to be a rustic retreat, or a building that can be used year-round. Electricity and lighting will have to be taken into account in your initial design, and a qualified electrician hired to undertake the work during the building process.

STEP THREE

PREPARING YOUR TREEHOUSE CONSTRUCTION KIT

Following is a comprehensive list of all the tools and equipment that you might need to construct your treehouse, some of these are items are absolutely vital, others less so. Again, if you have planned sufficiently you should know what you will need before you start.

IN YOUR TOOLBELT

pocket full of screws

bolts

stanley knife

screwdriver

tape measure

pencil

TOOLS

extension ladder

nylon rope with metal pulley

climbing harness

workbench

circular saw

cordless drill

sander

jigsaw or coping saw

mitre saw or a sharp handsaw

hammer

socket wrench

crowbar

chisel

adjustable square

hole cutter

spirit level

chalkline

paintbrushes

Notes

• When using outdoor power tools in wet weather whenever possible use battery-powered tools, as they are safer and do not have the associated problems of trying to move around a tree with cables back to the power source. When you take any tools up a tree always tie them to your belt with a lanyard, very few tools can survive being dropped from a height.

• Is your selected tree near enough to a power supply for your tools?

• How will you get the heavy timbers to the base of the tree?

• Have you somewhere to store tools and charge batteries out of the rain.

BUILDING MATERIALS

8" coach bolts and lag screws, stainless steel to prevent rusting and tree damage.

6" / 4" / 3" galvanized screws for your frame.

Decking screws for the internal flooring and external decking.

Joist hangers (one for each bracer—you'll find these at your local builder's supplier)

Metal plates to attach bracers to the treehouse.

8"x 3" softwood for the joists and platform.

4"x 2" softwood for the walls and windows.

3"x2" softwood for the roofing.

Ribbed hardwood for the decking and tongue-and-grooved (T & G) flooring for the interior.

Door and window handles and hinges.

Polycarbonate for windows.

T & G Lining board for inside walls.

Post-mix cement for treehouse stilts.

Insulating material such as polystyrene sheets.

Left: Constructing a treehouse may be one of the most challenging and rewarding activities you ever do. It's important to be well prepared in advance and to seek as much information as possible about how to look after your tree, how to be safe on site, and how to build a well-supported structure.

Notes

- Make sure the screws are guaranteed to a suitable weight for the load they will be bearing.

- Never use nails when fixing to a tree.

- Never use glass windows in a treehouse construction, it could break as the treehouse flexes in the wind and cause injury.

- Always use pressure treated wood and also apply two coats of a quality wood preservative to the completed treehouse for color and additional protection.

- The wood you use as your main building material should be both strong and lightweight to create a structure that does not put excessive pressure on your tree, such as pine (always pressure treated) or even bamboo or cedar.

STEP FOUR

DESIGNING A STRONG FOUNDATION FOR YOUR TREEHOUSE

Your platform gives definition to your treehouse, and is the most important structural part. Six feet off the ground should be adventurous enough for most small children, though adults or older children may wish to be higher off the ground. Just remember that the height of the platform will be determined by the strength and size of your tree and the position of its branches.

One of the simplest treehouse designs is to position the platform below the start of the tree's lower branches. You will then only have to tackle the main tree trunk coming through the floor, and you will only have to to incorporate branches into the walls and roof.

1. Once you have decided on your chosen tree, it is a very good idea to measure the branches and make an aerial plan of the tree and the direction of its limbs. This will help you to decide where to position your platform, and know where the tree trunk and branches will puncture the flooring and walls.

2. Work on the ground if possible, laying out the platform frame, and then hoisting it into the tree using your pulley. In order to raise a platform, there must be at least three level points where a platform can be attached, and most good sites have four points.

3. In complicated trees you may have to assemble or part-assemble the frame actually in the tree. Either way it is vital that before you begin bolting the platform to the tree that you make sure that the platform is precisely level. Bolt one end of the frame to the tree and use your spirit level to find an exact angle to bolt the rest of the platform to the tree.

4. There are a number of methods for fixing the platform:
   a. If your chosen tree is strong enough to support the weight of the entire treehouse, then you'll want to use knee bracers (45 degree metal supports) attached to the tree trunk to hold it in place. You can use ropes attached

to the topmost branches of the tree to support the beams until the bracers are put into place below. Knee bracers are bolted into the heartwood of the tree using base blocks. When bolting the platform to the tree, don't strip the bark all the way around at any time, as this will harm the tree. Make sure that the bolts are staggered and not attached beside each other, as this can also damage the tree. It will assume that the two wounds you have given it are one, and the wood in between the two bolts will die

Above: **Almost finished the platform! The flooring has been laid, and the treehouse is nearly ready to receive the wall frames. On the ground, blue tarpaulin covers the grass to protect it from damage during the build.**

and rot away, leaving your treehouse to destabilize. You will also want to stagger your bracers around the tree so that no two are bolted onto the tree at the same height . This will give you more stability, and is better for the health of the tree.

b. For less strong trees, support may be provided partially or wholly by the use of stilts, giving your treehouse solid legs that are fixed into the ground with post-mix cement. Soak the ends of the stilts overnight in wood preservative and wrap them in waterproof membrane, then set them into a dug hole below the frost line, at least two or three feet deep on a bed of hardcore, and pour in cement.

c. A "floating-point" method of attaching your platform is best when dealing with more than one tree at a time. Trees move independently of each other, so if fixed joints are used to attach the main beams to both trees they may stress and damage both tree and treehouse. By using a fixed point on one tree and a floating point on the other, the platform acts very much like a suspension bridge, able to move as the trees sway.

d. An easier way to assemble a treehouse platform without worrying too much about needing a floating point load system is to cantilever the beams outward from a single trunk supported by knee bracers underneath, like the spokes of a wheel. For a hexagonal treehouse you will want at least six floor beams each supported by a knee bracer. After you make sure the beams are level and secure, you can then lay the joists across the platform and form a solid frame. Note: trees may bend slightly and you will have to accommodate beam lengths accordingly.

e. An alternative, and trickier method of attachment for advanced builders is using a suspended-point load. Strong steel wires are attached to the ends of the platform beams and held in place from tree branches high up above the treehouse. Wooden blocks provide a rest for the steel

Right: Knee bracers are bolted to this tree trunk to form the supports for the platform. You can see that they join the tree at different levels– this is to ensure that the flow of sap in the tree is not cut off in any way, and is better for the health of the tree. The length of each knee bracer is cut to size so that they are all exactly level and meet at the same height, ready to support the platform.

cables and are bolted into the tree. If you are suspending the treehouse from cables, you must ensure that the cables do not dig into or strangle the branches. Never wrap cables directly around branches, and always leave a space for the tree to grow.

5. Once you have the basic platform frame up, you can lay the decking. Mark out where your walls will be. Where the platform decking meets your interior decking you must leave a small 5mm gap in the platform floor, all the way round underneath your walls, where water will drop down from the structure. The wall should cover both inside and outside flooring so you do not see the gap underneath. Infill the platform floor with pine flooring boards. The TreeHouse Company always use non-slip decking—the wood is ridged in neat lines and has an attractive finish. Use normal pine floorboards for the interior. After you have completed the platform, further building will be easier, as suddenly you will find that you have something to stand on while working in the tree. Still remember to always be tied on!

Notes

• Use long and wide supporting beams rather than lots of smaller ones. Wherever you attach the platform to the tree, weight will be dispersed.

• Make sure the branches you attach bolts to are a minimum of six inches in diameter (this is for the very simplest treehouse, try to make it at least ten inches diameter if you can).

STEP FIVE

BUILDING THE TREEHOUSE FRAME

Before you construct the wall frames, you will have to take into account where the door and any windows will be situated. You will also need to provide room for the door and window jambs and fix these to the wall frame before assembling.

You'll want to stay firmly on the ground for as long as possible when constructing the wall frames for your treehouse. Use your pulley to lift as much as you can of the completed treehouse into the air, including fitted windows and doors if weight allows. However, you will also have to take into consideration whether any of the tree branches are going to protrude through your walls. You may have to hoist the

wall into the tree, affix it to your platform and then scribe the plywood and covering boards around any branches going through the walls, remembering to leave a good gap for the branch to keep on growing.

The wall frames have to consist of straight lines to give them strength. Remember that triangular shapes give extra support, so use triangles wherever possible in your frame. For a simple four-sided treehouse you will have four wall frames and two panels that will frame your gable roof. That means the two end frames will have a triangular shape at the top, and the two side frames will be rectangular. For the Treehouse for all Seasons (see page 136), The TreeHouse Company

Left: This tiny building almost seems more tree than house. At this stage, with the "see through walls" you can really picture what your final interior space is going to look like. Little children will find it magical being so close to the branches of the tree.

Left: After framing the covering can be fixed leaving plenty of room around all of the branches protruding through the walls.

Left: Shingling is quite a complex way of covering the exterior of the treehouse. However, the cedar used will give the outside of this round treehouse a rustic and magical look that is well worth the extra effort.

Above: "Waney" edge timber covering makes a natural looking treehouse, in this case picked out with a contrasting green timber trim.

Above: Applying shingles to any wall will give texture and interest.

used a longer rear wall to create a trapezium shaped treehouse with a sloping roof. Whatever dimensions you have chosen, you will want to check them carefully here.

1. Decide which walls are going to be your "by" walls (these will be the two opposite walls that sandwich your "butt" walls). By walls can have a corner trim, and butt walls will need to be cut slightly shorter to fit between the by walls.

2. Once you have your frames constructed, attach the doors and windows (see section 7) before covering the exterior of the frame.

3. Plywood sheathing can be used to cover the frame. Whether you are covering the frame with shingles, horizontal or vertical weatherboard, you will still need something to nail it to. Your exterior covering is worth a bit of thought, as it can really dictate the look of the treehouse. Some of the photographs shown in the book may inspire you, or you may have your own ideas. How about using slices of trunk and branch ends to cover your treehouses in lots of little circles for a natural look, or even using an electric router on weatherboard to create wavy edges, and staining the finished product a bright and vivid color?

4. Insulation is a good idea even if you are not intending to install heating or electricity in your treehouse. Polystyrene sheets can be layered against the inside frame, and then covered with a roll of polythene as a vapor barrier.

5. Finally your interior lining board can be nailed on top, or smooth tongue-and-groove boards or even sheets of woven bamboo for a really smart finish.

STEP SIX
CONSTRUCTING THE ROOF

For our treehouse we will construct a sloping roof rather than a flat roof as it has three advantages: it is far easier to keep your treehouse waterproofed, you will have no additional weight on the structure from leaves or snow, and it is certainly more aesthetically pleasing. Your roof should have a good overhang (minimum six inches) so that rainfall will not spill down the walls. Remember to use a safety harness attached as high up in the tree as possible while working on the roof! It is also a good idea to attach any tools you are using to the treehouse or a tree branch by rope so that if you drop them they won't hit anyone standing below the structure, and you can pull them back up again with ease.

If you want to get fancy with advanced roofing techniques, check out some of The TreeHouse Company's ideas—porch roofing over the door, six-sided pagodas, triangular thatching, skylights, and even roofs with conical peaks.

1. Calculate the pitch (slant) of your roof using string. (Ask someone to hold a string frame in place while you check the slant of the roof.)

Above: **Where a branch or trunk comes through a roof a floating neoprene collar is used to allow for growth, expansion, and movement as well as keeping the interior dry.**

It shouldn't be too steep or you will find it hard to balance while laying the roof tiles A pitch of 20 to 30 degrees is recommended.

2. The frame of your walls should account for where the roof will be attached. You can have two sets of protruding timbers at each end of your treehouse, and one of these ends will form your door jambs. From these you can start to form your ridgepole and all the right-angled triangles that will make up a two-sided sliding roof.

3. Lay 2" x 2" timbers across the slant of the walls. Then for extra support you'll need to fill in joists in between these struts and lay down plywood sheets on top. Screw these down, don't nail them to the structure.

4. The area where your tree branches come through the roof needs to be treated carefully. Use collars of neoprene (like rubber wetsuit material) around the branches to waterproof the roof. This will allow the tree to expand and grow while fitting tightly.

5. After the collars have been fitted, shingle from the bottom up and around the branches. The TreeHouse Company often tend to use cedar shingles for their exterior roofing; this can be quite expensive, but they look completely natural, weather beautifully, are lightweight, and are guaranteed for thirty years. Cedar has its own natural oil and so does not need to be treated. Attach each shingle with two nails. A less expensive alternative to cedar is using strips of felt shaped tiles, which can be laid using felt tacks.

6. Some people prefer the rustic look of exposed roof beams, but others may wish to run a fascia around where the walls meet the roof to cover exposed beams. You can carve this fascia to match the style of your treehouse, and paint or stain it.

Above: There are lots of different types of roofing to choose from, but do remember not to use heavy materials. These red and green felt tiles are ideal for treehouse use, as they are both light and rain resistant. Shaped tiles can be used to create a patterned roof, crowning the treehouse with a bit of charm.

Above: A fascia will hide exposed beams and give a really neat finish to the treehouse—scalloped-edge fascias like this one can be made simply, using the bottom of a paint pot to draw out semi-circles on the wood.

Above: Small details such as this oriental style ridge beam give interest to any treehouse.

Above: When shingling a large roof, start at the bottom and work your way up the tree trunk. An occupation not suitable for those afraid of heights. Don't forget the safety harness!

Notes

• Don't design the roof sloping down toward the door—the last thing you'll want is to get soaked every time you go in and out of the treehouse.

• Don't use heavy slate or clay tiles on the roof.

STEP SEVEN

INSTALLING WINDOWS AND DOORS

Windows and doors should be considered at an early stage and spaces left in the wall frames for them during construction. You may be able to use reclaimed window frames from salvage yards, or even buy new ones, but if not, you can always make them yourself on site—just remember never to use real glass in a treehouse window, if a branch hits against it then it could cause some serious damage. Always use polycarbonate windows, which are unbreakable.

WINDOWS

1. If you are using standard 3 "x 2" timber for your wall frames then you can also use this for the windows. You'll need to groove the sides length-wise to create a gap where the polycarbonate can be fixed.

2. Put a line of silicon down each side in between the wood and the window to waterproof. Put in beading so that it fits neatly back in to hold the window and screw into place.

3. You'll want the bottom of your window to have a slanting sill with a small indent running the length of the underside to stop rainwater backtracking onto the structure. Attach the frame together with screws and wood glue.

4. On the outside edge of your polycarbonate glass, seal the window with a line of clear silicon all the way round where the edge meets the wood. It is best to stain your windows before they are fitted.

DOORS

In the Treehouse for all Seasons (see page 136), the door entrance was made by stepping through the fork of the branches and fitting the door in the gap; this is quite a sophisticated approach, and unless you have two boughs with the correct spacing, you will probably want to try a different method. It is generally easier to incorporate the door space into the frames of your wall and roof

Far left: Just like normal house building, you can design your treehouse to have some special features such as this lovely cedar shingled dormer window. The window frame is built into the main structure of the building, and also supported underneath by mini knee-bracers.

Left: An unusual use of polycarbonate made the walls of this treehouse completely see-through, creating a bright and airy space that is given privacy by a willow hurdle balustrade.

Above: A simple log effect door with a small window allows the occupants to see who is visiting the treehouse.

Above: The simplest of arched doors can be beautifully stained and stencilled to give a special touch to the finished treehouse.

area. Like windows, reclaiming doors is a cost-effective and environmentally friendly approach, but you can also make your own doors. Once you have mastered the technique of fitting doors ten feet up in the air, you can get fancy with the details, carving out spyholes, fitting nice locks and handles, and even stencilling the door.

1. The best time to make a door is after the floor has been laid, so that you can cut the door to fit your platform. Always maintain your ninety degree corner angles, make sure the diagonal measurements are equal and account for a small gap for movement of the door.

2. Fit hinges to the doorjambs on your wall frames so that after the walls are in place you can hoist up the door and slide it into place. An inward opening door is best as it takes up less room on your deck.

Right: This doorway is hidden behind a tree branch. Inward opening, with custom made fleur-de-lis emblems on a silver-gray background, the door gives a secretive feeling to the treehouse entrance.

STEP EIGHT
BALUSTRADES, LADDERS, AND STAIRCASES

A treehouse balcony is the perfect place to sit and sip drinks in the open air with a beautiful view all around as the sun goes down. Alternatively you can build a second structure in another tree and use this as your outdoor deck (see Section Nine on Accessories for tips on building rope-bridges between trees). If you are creating a treehouse for children, the importance of making a strong barrier between your little ones and a nasty fall is obvious, but balustrades can also be an attractive feature on your treehouse. There are several options of entry and exit that also need to be considered, from adventurous and tricky rope-ladders to easily accessed staircases.

Above: A ladder now commonly used in children's treehouse design, the double-rung ladder is more secure and easier to climb. It was originally made for a little boy who was frightened that wolves would be able to enter his treehouse. Luckily everyone knows that wolves can't climb double-rung ladders.

Above: The most challenging treehouse entrance of all is the rope ladder. Safely secured at both ends, it's a way of adding some of that Swiss Family Robinson feeling to a children's play area.

Right: Real twig balustrades can look amazing on treehouse balconies, just remember to use reclaimed wood and check that each branch is sound and free from decay, as all balustrades must above all form a safe supportive barrier.

BALUSTRADES

Balustrades should be a minimum height of thirty inches for an adult, and may be slightly less for children, depending on their height. The height of your balcony railing will depend upon the height of the user—for example a taller rail might be nice for an adult to lean an elbow on, but this would be too high for a child to see over! Banister rails should be placed close enough that a four inch round ball (the size of an infant's head) cannot pass between them.

To construct your balustrade drill through the floorboards with a hole cutter to make a round hole in the platform frame for the balustrade posts to sit. Bolt these posts securely to the platform frame. Rails should be attached to the inside of the corner posts so that if the nails come loose the railings will not collapse if leaned out upon.

There are plenty of design options, such as picket fence, crosshatch, or even balusters made from branches gathered from the garden with the bark still intact. Screw down the branches through the top horizontal and then the bottom horizontal. The "real wood" balustrades visually tie the house back to the tree and its surroundings.

Ladders

Ladders need to be strong and are best fixed into the ground with cement using the same method as stilts (see Section Four) and bolted into the tree or treehouse platform at the top. You should use six screws to fix each tread, hammered through the rails and into the sides of the steps. Use four inch or six inch bolts for extra strength. If you are using rounded rungs, it is a great idea to fit double rungs to act as handholds; these are much safer and easier to use, particularly for children. Fixing a handrail will help to give extra support while climbing.

As well as being much easier to construct rope-ladders have the advantage that they can be pulled up into the tree to give the building privacy and security.

Whatever you do, don't nail boards to the trunk and use these as stairs—they won't last very long and are bound to cause a nasty accident as well as damaging the tree.

Staircases

Staircases should have well-supported treads, so it is a good idea to fit metal corner brackets underneath them. However, if you feel that incorporating metal into your treehouse spoils the look, you can fit wooden blocks instead of corner brackets.

Spiral staircases are obviously a more complex method of entry, but look enormously attractive. They are formed using a central pole concreted into the ground, with the treads fitted into the pole using huge bolts and eyebolts.

Above: Steps should be wide and easy to climb, securely attached to the main frame of the treehouse. Likewise, balustrades are fixed to the platform, with strong railings tall enough to protect someone from a fall if they should accidentally slip.

Above: The most complex method of entry to build, the spiral staircase is nonetheless a dramatic and luxurious way for adults to reach their tree-top house. This one is wide enough to safely carry a tray of drinks or box of toys upstairs, with a coconut rope handrail for balance. Here you can see how the spiral staircase is constructed, with each staircase tread attached to the main pole using eye sockets and strong bolts.

STEP NINE
ACCESSORIES

Half the fun of your finished treehouse is when you add all the great accessories. Everyone loves to swing in the shade of a tree on a lazy summers day, and basket pulleys are great for hoisting up picnics for adults and children alike. Adventurous play can be had with zip slides or a fireman's pole, while rope-bridges allow you to connect your treehouse to other tree-decks.

BASKET PULLEYS

Your balcony or corner balustrade can hold a beam of wood, or wood carved pulley holder to hoist up a basket. It is better that you attach the pulley above head height so that you don't have to lean over the balcony to collect the basket. Attach a metal swivel-eye to your treehouse with screws. Feed the rope through the pulley and fasten to a snap hook to hold the basket. The other end of the rope can be held in place by a metal cleat attached to the inside of the railing, so you can wind the rope up and down as you would with any normal household blind.

ZIP SLIDES

For a smooth ride use a steel pulley with two rollers and strong cable clamps. Allow enough slack in the steel cable so that the rider will travel uphill at the end of the journey. Attach the cable to wooden buffer blocks using strong screws and onto the tree trunk well above your launching platform. Anchor the cable to the faraway tree on a strong side branch rather than the main trunk, to avoid hitting the tree at the end of the ride. A good way of providing a launching platform is to fix a gate on your deck, which can be securely bolted shut when the zip slide is not in use.

SWINGS

Take a piece of 2"x 6" pine and drill two sets of holes through the top of the sanded plank. Feed nylon rope through the two holes at each side and tie using bowline knots. Make sure the seat is level and then fix the top of the ropes to a strong main branch of the tree also using

Above: A simple rope, pulley, and basket allows for essential supplies to be hoisted up into the treehouse.

Left: A new twist on an old theme. Basket pulleys are great for hoisting up wine and supplies for treehouse picnics, but this one also has its own duck overlooking the lake below.

Right: Rope bridges give the illusion of being construction from natural materials like wood and rope, but they also use metal chains to give a strong support for all those children who love endlessly running across from tree to tree.

Far right: For the really adventurous a "crows nest" viewing platform can be installed high above the treehouse.

bowline knots. Use neoprene collars to buffer the tied-on ropes, so as not to damage the tree during its growth. Alternatively, a button swing can be constructed with just one piece of rope suspended from the tree and going through the middle of a round, nicely sanded wooden seat and knotted underneath. You may also be able to fit swings suspended from the underside of your treehouse platform if it sits high enough from the ground.

ROPE BRIDGES

The easiest site for a rope bridge is between two strong trees with surrounding platforms. The edges of the two platforms need to be facing each other exactly parallel. Measure across with string to determine how much chain linkage you will need. Chains will be attached around the trunks of both trees and require a little slack in between to give leeway. Use bolts with washers then nuts with washers through the chain link into wood blocks to brace against the trees. Straight slip-proof

ridged decking is most suitable for your slats, and these can also be screwed through the chain links and spaced evenly to form the base of the rope bridge. Two sets of ropes then need to be attached to your balustrade posts at either end of the bridge, top and bottom, and rope wound up and down in triangles to form a safe barrier. When you have to cut your rope, remember that you will need to bind the ends with knots to prevent fraying.

Fireman's Pole

For a quick exit, cut out a circular hole in your decking large enough for a child to fit through. Place a three inch diameter strong aluminum pipe in the center of the hole with one end attached to your treehouse structure or supporting tree branch and the bottom end securely fixed into the ground with post-mix cement. Next fit a trapdoor, or shape a hinged "lid" for the pole hole to avoid any accidents, with the lid opening upward only. Leave a cut in the lid so that it can be raised open to free the pole for use. You can also have a fireman's pole at the side of the treehouse and gain access to it by opening a gate in the balustrades.

Above: People always say that being up a treehouse in strong winds is like sailing on a boat. So why not encourage the illusion a little further?

STEP TEN

TREEHOUSE INTERIORS

FURNITURE

Now that you have a wonderfully constructed treehouse, you will want to furnish the interior for adult or children's use. Here are some popular ideas.

If you intend to use the treehouse interior as a sleepover space, you can build a raised bunk bed area close to the ceiling—perfect if you have also installed a sky-light to watch the stars at night and the birds during the day. If space is more limited, you can attach wooden pull-down bed frames to the walls using hinges and chains. These can also serve as seats for extra guests. Window seats are also popular, particularly in bay windows, and these can also provide good storage space underneath. Mirrors are perfect for making any treehouse interior seem more spacious, and can be constructed with carved branch frames that look like something out of Snow White.

What, though, could be more magical than having your own wooden furniture specially made to match your tree? The TreeHouse Company furniture can be ordered through the company, made by an Ayrshire woodcraftsman. The Little Sapling TreeHouse furniture range includes child-size stools and picnic-tables, adult dining-tables, porch seats, and full-length cabinets. The wooden chests are loved by both adults and children. Adults use them as stylish coffee tables, while children love them because they look like old pirate chests. They can be fitted with a cushion and used as a storage seat, or even used to hide away toys and games.

The smallest of details in accessories such as button swings can be made to fit the spirit of the tree by using carved wood that gives a rustic look. After all, it is harder for a child to imagine that they are in a pirate ship or medieval look-out tower when they have plastic tables

Right: **Rustic furniture complements the treehouse beautifully.**

Left: A simply lined interior gives a very polished look.

Below left: If your proposed treehouse is going to be used for sleepovers, you may wish to consider installing permanent bunk beds like these to the interior. Plan your layout accordingly, and remember that if your interior space is precious, you can create a loft area for sleeping up near the eaves.

and chairs to use. Little Sapling furniture has a more organic feel—even the little stools look like mushrooms that have sprung naturally from the treehouse floor.

If you prefer to make your own furniture, make simple stools by using the cut-off ends from tree trunks, remembering of course to sand the surfaces down to avoid splinters. Unlined walls can be a quirky way of providing small shelving spaces on the frame of the treehouse. Tree branches sliced lengthways with the bark intact and supported by brackets also lend a more organic feel.

INTERIOR DECORATION

A PLAYROOM FOR CHILDEN

Transform the inside of the treehouse into a cozy den for children using rugs and bean-bags. You can add on pretty features such as internal shutters or sew tailor-made treehouse curtains for the windows—chocolate brown material with little doors and windows appliquéd on and a leafy green pelmet added. When open, the curtains look like two trees, and when closed, like a treehouse. Window boxes for children can be placed on the outside or inside window-sills,

Above: Permanent fixtures like this toy chest are worth planning ahead to incorporate in the interior space. Unlined walls can also make fascinating alcoves to decorate and store small goods.

Right: This handmade art-glass window gives a lovely effect when light cathes it at the right angle.

and if you use pretty gravel and faux-flowers, they won't need any further attention.

The floor can be sanded and polished and stenciled, for example with leaf patterns. Stencils of birds, flowers, or even train tracks and roads for playing cars and trucks, will also be a lot of fun for small children. Or you can section off an area of floor in a small area such as a corner or bay window and elevate it using MDF framed boxing. With a curtain rail across your "stage," storage underneath for costumes and make-up, and a full-length mirror for admiring their reflections, the children will have everything they need for their Treehouse Theater Company.

There are as many exciting features for adventurous minds as your imagination can produce. Create a secret message display by transforming a two-door key holder box. Spray chalkboard paint on the back of the box to give an area that can be chalked over, and leave

Above: With some care a table can be
scribed around the tree trunk its self.
A great place for homework!

Above left: You can transform your treehouse interior into a bright and welcoming place with some simple soft furnishings and decorations.

Above: Always try to let plenty of light enter the treehouse to make it welcome and attractive.

Left: This simple bed / seating area is made from some marine plywood and the off cuts of the 5″ posts used as supports for the staircase.

Left: Soft furnishings and fabrics will always complement the treehouse but take care not to let these become damp.

colored chalk inside. Alternatively, blackboard spray can be used directly onto your inside walls. A flagpole with embroidered pirate flag or family crest on it looks great on the deck, and for little ones, a rocking horse is the perfect place to ride into the sunset. For lazy days, a stow-away hammock can be attached to hooks on opposite walls.

INTERIOR DECORATION

THE ADULT RETREAT

Pale colors do wonders for small spaces, but bright white can be a little harsh, so try some soft apricots or tinted creams. Let your color palette reflect the personality of your tree. The African Treehouse interior (see page 100) was pale to match their silver birches, but if your treehouse is lucky enough to be situated in the arms of a red horse chestnut tree, you might want to add a splash of their vivid pink blooms to your interior colors.

Carpeting can be the ultimate luxury in soft furnishing, however, do test your treehouse for any possible drips and leaks before you install anything too expensive. Most people prefer a natural wooden floor, with rugs to take the edge off winter chill.

If you have installed electricity and heating, lighting can add drama or subtlety to any space (uplights and dimmer switches give you greater control of the ambience of your interior than a single light-switch). Candles look fantastic inside treehouses, but don't forget that you are in a wooden, flammable structure, never leave candles unattended and always place them on a proper surface. You can use individual terracotta saucers to hold tea-lights and then sit them welcomingly on your treehouse staircase to guide guests to the table, or even fit uplights onto your lawn. A large mirror on one wall doubles your space and reflects candlelight.

Large windows often provide an excellent greenhouse effect, and bringing in flowers and plants ensures a real link between the environment outside and living space within. It is also a good idea to place wooden nesting boxes in the higher limbs of the tree and provide food for the birds, as this will attract them to your treehouse. You can also suspend lanterns from the tree branches outside for a really mystical effect.

Left: This treehouse is rather unusual as the entire interior and exterior walls have been covered using bamboo. It gives a light warmth and golden glow to the building, as well as an exotic feel to this luxurious treehouse. Hollow bamboo pipes act as beams for this thatched treehouse.

INDEX